# BROWNS
## Scrapbook

# BROWNS Scrapbook

## A Fond Look Back at Five Decades of Football

## CHUCK HEATON

GRAY & COMPANY, PUBLISHERS
CLEVELAND

Gray & Company, Publishers
www.grayco.com

Library of Congress Cataloging-in-Publication Data

Heaton, Chuck.
Browns scrapbook : A Fond Look Back at Five Decades of Football, from a Legendary Cleveland Sportswriter / Chuck Heaton.
  p. cm.
ISBN-13: 978-1-59851-043-0 (softcover)
1. Cleveland Browns (Football team : 1946-1995)—History.
2. Heaton, Chuck.   3. Sports journalism—Ohio—Cleveland.
4. Plain dealer (Cleveland, Ohio : 1961) I. Title.
GV956.C6H43 2007
796.332'640977132—dc22      2007029583

Printed in the United States of America
10 9 8 7 6 5 4 3 2 1

*To Cece*
*My Wife*
*My Love*
*My Life*

# Contents

# Foreword

CHUCK HEATON WAS THE first sportswriter to greet me when I walked gingerly into the *Plain Dealer* sports department as a summer intern in 1979. I was 22 and awestruck.

We all have heroes at that age. Mine did not play sports but wrote about them. My brother and I plotted nearly every morning to beat the other to the front door and the *Plain Dealer* sports pages. I read everything Chuck Heaton wrote from the time I could remember reading. And now he was standing in front of me with a warm smile, this dapper gentleman, extending his hand and welcoming me to the PD sports department. What a thrill.

Little did I know that that was the way Chuck Heaton treated everyone who crossed his path.

As I embarked on assignments on the road, I found that Chuck Heaton's name was synonymous with the *Plain Dealer* in the sporting world. It opened doors for a young reporter learning the ropes. Many of my early interviews for the *Plain Dealer* ended with the subject saying something like, "You tell Chuck Heaton I said hello and to give me a call."

I had the honor of working alongside this great role model for 14 years. He touched co-workers and athletes a way in which they never forgot him. When Leroy Kelly was voted to the Pro Football Hall of Fame 1994, he chose Chuck Heaton to present him for induction. At the time, Chuck was only the third sportswriter in 31 years to serve as a presenter.

Chuck's professional accomplishments were exceeded only by the accomplishments in his daily life. His dedication to God and his devotion to his faith were apparent to anyone who knew him. In 14 years, I never heard him speak a cross word of anyone. As a kid reading the sports page, Chuck Heaton was one of my heroes. To have a hero exceed your expectations is a remarkable thing.

—Tony Grossi

# Editor's Note

Most of these articles were originally written by my father for a retrospective series titled "Browns Scrapbook" that ran in the *Plain Dealer* from 1991 to 1993—shortly before he retired after 51 years as a sportswriter. A few contain passing references to contemporary events of the early 1990s (including fond words for Art Modell, who would break fans' hearts by moving the team to Baltimore just a couple of years later). Still, these stories stand timeless as a memoir of the "old Browns" told by a sportswriter who came to know the team and its players better than anyone over those five decades.

—Michael Heaton

# PLACES

# Spirit of Togetherness
# Permeated Camps at Hiram

"NOT EVEN A BEER joint in this town."

That was the comment of Preston Carpenter in 1956 to a woman standing next to him as they looked out the window of a sitting room in the Centennial Dormitory at Hiram College.

Katie Brown just smiled in reply. She probably never told her husband—coach Paul Brown—about this initial reaction of the running back, the first draft pick from Arkansas.

The Browns spent 26 summers in that bucolic, beerless spot, and I was with them for 24 of those years. It all started for me on a warm Sunday afternoon in 1954 after a drive down Route 82 from Cleveland.

My car radio was tuned to an Indians doubleheader against the New York Yankees from the Stadium. The Tribe had been my first sports love since joining the *Plain Dealer* eight years earlier.

The club was on its way to win 111 games and the American League pennant. But my assignment had been changed and I was being tried out as the Browns beat writer.

In assigning me to the Browns beat a few days earlier, *Plain Dealer* Sports Editor Gordon Cobbledick warned: "We'll see what kind of a job you do. This is a very important beat."

Never did I think that it would be so much fun, or that this would become an assignment that would occupy most of my working days for 24 years.

Memories of those summers at Hiram College and Kent State University flood back each year as Cleveland's pro football team prepares for another training camp.

Hiram College and the quiet town at the intersection of Routes 82 and 700 turned out to be a second home. The media people were housed with the players in those days and usually went home only on weekends.

Nothing ever will quite duplicate the togetherness that was prevalent at Hiram.

It probably started with the people at the college. Bill Hollinger was athletic director and basketball coach. But during many of those summer months, he was the unofficial host of the Browns.

One of the fine people in athletics, he worked closely with Paul Brown and then with Blanton Collier and Nick Skorich, the head coaches of the team during that tenure. He did all in his power to make the days glide by smoothly, whether it was by lining the field or hosting a social hour.

His daughters even pitched in as hostesses. They often worked in the cafeteria.

Dr. Elmer Jagow was president of the college during most of those years. A pleasant, interesting man, he could be found on the sidelines at practice for some part of almost every afternoon.

It was at Hiram that the two greatest players in the history of the team—quarterback Otto Graham and fullback Jim Brown—trained. Graham came out of a brief retirement to rejoin the club at Hiram in 1955 for his last season.

Graham hadn't practiced or played for more than a year when he returned that August, but he stepped back in as the starter immediately. As I stood behind the offense and watched him throw that first morning in that first practice, I noted only one sign of age. There was a faint bald spot beginning to show at the back of his head.

Jim Brown arrived on the scene two years later and also after practice was well under way. He drove up in a fire engine red convertible after an all-night trek from Chicago, where he had played in the College All-Star Game. Brown also immediately became the starting fullback.

Nature took care of watering the solitary football field for the most part. It occasionally became rock hard, however, and if the players complained enough, trainer Leo Murphy and equipment manager Morrie Kono solved the problem by buying the Garrettsville firefighters a few drinks. The volunteers would drive their trucks to Hiram and do some late-night watering with hoses attached to the two fire hydrants near the field.

The menu has changed considerably through the years, but one characteristic of all camps from Bowling Green to Berea has been excellent food. Preparation always has been by the school cafeteria workers, but top-drawer products always have been purchased without regard to cost.

The kitchen at Centennial Hall was not a large one, so on "steak night," the T-bones or porterhouses were char-broiled outside.

"One of my best memories of Hiram is walking up the hill from the field and smelling those steaks," former all-pro offensive tackle Dick Schafrath said. And Schafrath, now a state senator, was one of those who could down two or three of them for dinner.

Hiram did have the Hub, where a player could get ice cream or a soft drink and listen to a juke box, as well as a barber shop and post office. But beer was available not too far away. Practices usually were followed by caravans of cars to Garrettsville, a mile down the road, where alcohol was available. There also was the Aurora Inn to the west and the Welshfield and the Red Horseshoe Inn to the north. The coaches didn't encourage the beer runs, but they privately admitted that replenishing the body fluids after a long, hot workout was not a bad idea.

Leo and Morrie were up early and about their jobs. The days sometimes ended for them late in the afternoon when after practice they would drive over to nearby Garretsville, G-Ville as it was called by the players, to have a beer or two before dinner. Then they would return to work if needed, and they usually were.

Paul Brown was an early to bed guy. His meetings with the assistant coaches finished promptly at 9 p.m. and he was tucking up the covers before 10. That's when his aides, usually accompanied by some of the media, would tiptoe by his door at the end of the corridor and relax with a beer or two.

The late Ralph Hunter was the primary mover in bringing

the Browns to Hiram College for summer workouts. A friend of Paul Brown, he heard that the team was thinking of leaving their training quarters at Bowling Green.

The Browns had worked there since the team was formed in 1946, its first year in the All-America Conference. Bowling Green seemed an ideal spot with it dormitories, classrooms and fields.

There was one drawback. The distance from Cleveland was about 100 miles of country roads, and few fans saw the club until the start of the season.

Brown wanted a spot about an hour away from Cleveland proper—close enough to visit but too far for his charges to sample the delights of the bright lights. He found Hiram, smaller than Bowling Green but with all the other requirements.

The team went to the new training site down Route 82 for the first time in 1952 as a test. It stayed for 23 summers.

Eventually, when rosters were expanded, more room was needed for practice and housing, and the Hiram dorms weren't air conditioned. So the club moved on to Kent State University.

The summers at Hiram are remembered fondly by many, even by some of the players. They also are recalled as a spot of successful preparation for the season. The team had just two losing seasons in those 23 years.

# Kids Were Part of the Camp Scene

I REMEMBER ONCE THINKING that something seemed to be missing at the Browns training camp at Lakeland Community College, but I couldn't put my finger on it. It came to me when wives of the players gathered for "family day" with swarms of children all over the place. The kids had been absent earlier. Not the ones who pushed against the restraining ropes and pleaded for a handshake, an autograph or even a smile. They were there in large numbers hot or chilly, rain or shine.

Not on hand were sons and daughters of the coaches, the front office folks, the media or even those of some of the veteran players. They used to be around in rather large numbers when the Browns were doing their summer exercises at Bowling Green State University, Hiram College and even Kent State University.

Kids were all over. They had the run of those camps. Locker rooms weren't off limits and some of the boys might even be found showering with the players after practice. The girls, like my daughters Sharon and Alice, got their kicks from working on the food serving line, seeing the athletes up close and being amazed when trenchermen such as Dick Schafrath would ask for three steaks.

There were few restrictions. Everyone ate in the dormitory dining halls at the same time. Complaints were at a minimum, but occasionally a player would gripe that all the freshly baked chocolate chip cookies were gone before he was ready for dessert.

The kids knew where Art Modell's room was with the door always open. They all had been informed of the rule. He always left a handful of change on the dresser and they were welcome to use it for pop or a candy bar.

The ball boys of those years are grown now with some still in sports. Bert Jones, son of offensive coordinator Dub Jones, went on to quarterback the Baltimore Colts.

Casey Coleman has followed in the footsteps of his dad, Ken, to become the sports anchor at Channel 8.

Casey and other kids used to get involved in Wiffle ball games with Paul Warfield, who passed up a baseball career to sign with the Browns, and other players. "They usually would end by someone hitting the ball on to the roof of the dormitory," Casey recalled recently. "I also remember that I could throw a football farther than Bert Jones at that time in our lives."

Modell's nephew, Dick Rosen, was a regular for several summers. Figuring to make a few points with the owner, I asked him along on a drive to pick up daughter Allie at a Madison (O.) CYO camp. They were getting along famously for a brief time until Allie, subject to car sickness, lost her breakfast and a bottle of orange pop in Dick's lap. I had to take him salmon fishing on the Columbia river later that summer during a trip to Portland to make up for the mishap. Rosen, who quickly acquired the tag of "Flip" because of having the same name as an Indians star of the time—Al Rosen, who was nicknamed Flip—now is a success in business in New York City.

Paul Brown's sons, Mike and Pete, now general manager and personnel director, respectively, with the Cincinnati Bengals, both spent much time on the sideline at Hiram practices. Pete and I usually cut the squad in the early days of camp and bet a soda or two on who might be the most accurate. He usually won, but I suspect he might have had some inside information.

My son Mike was at Hiram annually. One summer he gave me a big scare. He had been home only a few days after a visit when my late wife, Pat, called with tears in her voice. "Mike has the mumps," she said. "Do you think some of the players will catch them?"

My first impulse was to keep mum, but finally I decided to confess to Modell and Dr. Vic Ippolito, then the team physician. I told them about all the time Mike spent in the locker room. Neither panicked.

"Chances are slim that anyone will get them," said the good doctor. He was right but not until I had some anxious hours. It was a good feeling of relief when camp ended with jaws bulging only from chaws of tobacco.

All in all, it was fun to have the kids around. Some players said it made the drudgery of camp more bearable.

# Green Hotel Was
# Lacking in Amenities

THE BROWNS GOT BOOKED into some fancy hotels through the years—Marriots, Hyatts, Hiltons, Stouffers—always top drawer.

Well, maybe not always. There was one glaring exception—the Green Hotel, as it was laughingly labeled, in Pasadena, Calif.

The Browns stayed at the Green usually about a week at a time. They used the hotel for about seven seasons.

The ugly, yellow brick building surrounded by pavement and with a minimum of elevators didn't have air conditioning—or even showers—in most rooms. The latter proved somewhat of a mixed blessing when the temperature rose into the 90s and flirted with 100 as it frequently did in August and September.

Some of the more clever athletes filled the tubs with cooling water. Then they deserted the lumpy mattresses for the home-made water bed.

The late Harold Sauerbrie was publicity man for the Browns at that time.

"I've found a small motel a few blocks from here," he said. "You're welcome to share the room with me, but don't tell anybody."

So we lived in comparative comfort that week while the others suffered.

One wing of the hotel was an old folks' home, where the 70-year-olds were referred to as "the kids." No matter how old they were, the residents enjoyed having the players so close.

In 1957, Bob Gain, a defensive tackle, with the meanness of a grizzly on the field and the nature of a teddy bear socially, became a quick favorite at the pool and in the lobby. To the "ooohs," "aaahs" and squeals of the residents, Gain would do belly flops off the high board into a postage stamp-sized pool.

Dick LeBeau was a rookie defensive back and was Gain's frequent companion in diving. LeBeau didn't make the final cut that summer, but he went on to an outstanding career with the Detroit Lions.

Sundown would find Gain hunched over a large table in the game room, two or three of his new friends at his side. He would be totally occupied with a jigsaw puzzle that covered the entire table top when completed.

Despite such diligence, Gain did not complete the puzzle during one weeklong stay. He found the puzzle in the same state 12 months later, waiting for him when he returned, but with new helpers.

Paul Wiggin, a defensive end who was to become captain of the Browns, has special memories of the hotel. Wiggin, who had recently married his college sweetheart, Carolyn, was trying to make the roster. He got his answer one afternoon when coach Paul Brown beckoned the Stanford graduate to the coaches table in the dining room. "You can tell Carolyn to get ready to come to Cleveland," Brown said quietly. Seated next to Brown, I had a minor exclusive story, but more importantly, the memory of the sheer joy on Wiggin's face.

Brown never explained why he picked the Green. He once mentioned its proximity to the Rose Bowl, where the team practiced.

A switch of hotels finally came after the Browns lost to the Rams. Superstitious, as are most football coaches, Brown probably blamed the loss on the Green.

Players who served some summers there have never forgotten the Green. It's sort of a badge of honor to be a survivor.

# Travel Incidents

DID YOU EVER LEND a millionaire $50? Or listen to one of the all-time best lines delivered by a legendary coach?

Or take off in a thunderstorm in a plane carrying its heaviest ever load? Or be present at an emergency landing because a football player was hyperventilating?

Those and many other such incidents will never be experienced by the present media covering the Browns. It was different back then.

Browns President Art Modell had to tap this writer for the money back in the early 1960s as the Browns waited for their plane to be repaired in the San Francisco airport. He had made the delay more pleasant by announcing to the squad, "The beers are on me."

Modell underestimated the thirst of a team just after a game. The beer disappeared faster than pizza at a teenager's party.

Reaching into my wallet for the "emergency" bill, I handed it over. Then came the saving call that the Browns' charter was boarding.

Browns coach Paul Brown wasn't in a very good mood after losing to the New York Giants in the late 1950's. It was not improved when the bus driver got lost on the way to LaGuardia Airport.

As the bus meandered about the countryside, the perspiring driver turned to Brown, sitting as usual in the front seat on the right, and apologized.

"I don't blame you," Brown said. "I blame the person who hired you." The players loved it.

In 1973, the team practiced for a week at Gold Rush Junction, an amusement park in Gatlinburg, Tenn., that was owned by Modell. At the end of the week, the Browns defeated the Atlanta Falcons in a game at the University of Tennessee in Knoxville.

Rain poured down throughout the exhibition. The equipment was soaking wet—and much heavier—as it was loaded on the plane. Vivid lightning and rolling thunder added to the picture as the team arrived at the Knoxville airport.

"You know this is the heaviest load I've ever taken off with," the pilot, looking rather nervous, confided to this uneasy passenger. But we made it home safely.

The Browns' charter had to refuel in Denver in 1971 on the way west. After the takeoff over the Rocky Mountains and through a thunderstorm of some violence, running back Reece Morrison began to hyperventilate. It quickly was discovered that there was no oxygen tank on board.

So at the request of Dr. Vic Ippolito, then the team physician, the pilot headed back to Denver. Morrison was taken to a hospital, where he quickly recovered. The players seemed less worried about his condition than going through that storm again.

It was on a flight to San Francisco in 1982 that Modell fainted. That was a prelude to his heart problem that has resulted in two bypass operations.

Hall of Fame fullback Marion Motley hadn't done much flying before joining the Browns in 1946. To feel more comfortable, he always draped a blanket over his head on takeoffs and landings.

The coaches, through most of my years of accompanying the team, usually sat in the tail section. Now, they occupy first class.

Modell mostly flies in a private plane now, but he and often his wife Pat used to fly with the club. So did some of the wives of the coaches starting with Blanton Collier's wife, Mary Forman. I still can see Collier sleeping peacefully with his head on Forman's shoulder after a victory.

I also remember Modell charging up the aisle from the back of the plane to chastise a player who was making a pass at a stewardess.

The media sat with the coaches and other front-office people in the back of the plane. For a number of years, they would find two well-iced beers in the seat, as did each player, on homecoming flights. Veterans loved to sit with non-drinking rookies.

Many more vignettes from my travels with the Browns come to mind. But most of all, I remember chats with a coach or player on the way to a game or the wonderful feeling that permeated the aircraft after a meaningful victory.

# Trip to Stillwater, Oklahoma Was Anything But Dull

THE BROWNS HAVE BEEN playing exhibitions in NFL home cities for a long time. It proved to be the profitable thing to do when home exhibitions were added to the season-ticket package by most clubs.

There were years, however, when the seal brown and orange uniforms were on display in such places as Akron; Toledo; Syracuse; Portland, Ore.; Birmingham, Ala.; Seattle; Memphis; South Bend, Ind.; Ann Arbor, Mich.; Columbus; Knoxville, Tenn.; Lincoln, Neb.; and Stillwater, Okla. Such barnstorming ended after a six-game exhibition slate in 1976 that began against the Baltimore Colts in Lincoln and ended against the Atlanta Falcons in Stillwater.

The Colts were the home team in Lincoln and won, 21-0. The pros received a rather cool reception in the home of the Cornhuskers with only 20,304 on hand.

The worst was yet to come, however. Bill Long, a scout for the Browns who made his home in Stillwater, persuaded the Cleveland brass that the city would be receptive to a pro game. The fact that he no longer works for the team has nothing to do with the six days spent in Stillwater.

Jerry Sherk, an all-pro defensive tackle for the Browns, had played at Oklahoma State in Stillwater. His appearance also was supposed to sell tickets.

The big jet plane, overloaded with players and equipment at this early point in the training season, landed about 10 p.m. in Stillwater. The landing was fine but the aircraft kept rolling and rolling until it finally stopped only a few feet short of a deep ravine.

It was reported later that this was the first plane of such size and with such a load to land at the airport. The sweat on the pilot's brow as he came down the steps on to the apron so attested.

A blast of hot, humid air was encountered as the door of the plane was opened. Despite the hour the thermometer read 99 degrees.

Taking this opportunity for an inexpensive vacation, Bill Scholl, then the Browns writer for the old *Cleveland Press*, and I had our wives along. Reservations had been made at the only luxury spa in town—a Holiday Inn.

We just settled in when an electrical storm hit. If you haven't experienced one on the plains, don't. The wind is like a hurricane, the lightning lights up a room and the thunder peals seem to hit the roof.

But it didn't cool off the city. The temperature never left the 90s until the day of the game, Saturday, when it dropped pleasantly into the 80s.

A restaurant called The Ancestors proved to be the only halfway decent eating place. So we had dinner there just about every night. The players quickly discovered that the town bars served only wine and beer.

Long came to the rescue of the media and team brass by hosting a cocktail party at his home and then taking the group to the Stillwater Country Club. It proved to be the highlight of the trip. There was some entertainment by Joe (Turkey) Jones, who displayed unexpected diving talent off the high board in the Oklahoma State pool.

On Saturday, a crowd announced as 24,227 showed up at the Oklahoma State field to see the Browns whip the Falcons, 31-7. It was as dull a game as most exhibitions are and the stadium was just about empty at the finish.

Sherk was introduced to cheers before the kickoff. But he had a strained leg muscle and didn't play.

Paul Hoynes, now the *Plain Dealer* baseball writer but then covering the Browns for the first time for the *Lake County News Herald*, traveled lightly. He carried all of his belongings for the week in a bowling bag. Probably having looked up the weather forecast, he didn't bring a sports coat. So he had to miss the one country club party—jackets were required.

Hoynes went down to the dressing room after the game as is the custom. Then he hustled to the press box to work but intended to return to Cleveland with the club.

When he finished his story and returned to the locker room he found it empty. The buses were on their way to Tulsa, the airline wisely deciding that it wouldn't try to make a takeoff on the short runway.

Only a few dollars in his pocket, Hoynes forlornly sat on a curb trying to decide what to do. The answer came in the form of a state police car with publicist Nate Wallack smiling from the front seat.

"You didn't think we'd leave without you, Hoynesy old boy," said Wallack. "We took a nose count."

The Scholls and the Heatons spent one more night at The Ancestors, drove a rented car to Tulsa the next morning and flew back to Cleveland.

"With all the expenses and the crowds we drew, we took a bath on that trip," team president Art Modell said.

# Trips West Always Special

HEADING WEST ALWAYS WAS special. There was a lot of talk about restaurants, talent shows, meeting old friends and touring the spots where they make the movies. In 1954 I went on my first plane ride as a member of the media. The Browns opened the exhibition season at Green Bay and then went west for three straight games—Los Angeles, San Francisco and Detroit at Dallas.

The airport was small in Green Bay and the trip attendant for Capitol Airlines was a bit uneasy.

"We've never landed on such a small field," the man told me. "It's going to be a test for our pilots."

The Browns landed safely and escaped with a 14-13 victory and set the stage for what they hoped would be another successful exhibition swing.

It wasn't to be.

The games in the Coliseum in L.A. and Kezar Stadium in San Francisco drew well, but that's all the Browns could say. They lost to the Rams, 38-10, and the 49ers, 38-21.

Coach Paul Brown wasn't feeling particularly well, either. He had been bitten by a fish during his Florida vacation and the poison took a long time to depart. So except for the daily practices, he spent most of his time in his room sleeping.

The squad stayed at St. Mary's College before the game against the 49ers and for a few days after. It was a great spot to practice but a poor place to socialize.

But when there's a will there's a way. The small town of Orinda was not too removed and boasted the Orinda Inn. It was there the media and the players would gather each night.

Abe Gibron was a guard on that team and a man who never has been beaten to a check. After the San Francisco defeat he still didn't complain.

"I don't know what he'll do but that little guy (Paul Brown) will find some way to win," said Gibron as he downed a beer. "He always does."

Brown said he talked to Gibron later when Abe became coach of the Chicago Bears. He asked him why he bought a car just like the one Brown owned—a brown Cadillac with all the extras.

"I knew it cost me too much, coach," Gibron replied. "And I knew you weren't paying me enough. The difference between the two cars is that mine was mortgaged for the next 10 years."

It was while at St. Mary's that defensive back Don Paul joined the team after having been traded by the Chicago Cardinals and Washington Redskins.

"He had some run-ins with his coaches, but we never found any evidence of it during his five years with the Browns," Brown once said.

Brown was the type of coach who pretended he didn't see what he disliked. Paul exited after bed check by a variety of means but never was seen by the coach.

After the loss in San Francisco and a few days of conditioning, the Browns traveled to Dallas. It was a rather long trip and they found that the heat had preceded them.

Black players were not allowed in the hotel the Browns used in Dallas and so the squad split up. The black players went to practice and then lived with black families in the area.

Game time came along soon enough. It was a disastrous one for Burrell Shields, a John Carroll graduate. He was given a complete lesson by Doak Walker, now in the football Hall of Fame in Canton. The Browns lost to the Lions, 56-31.

So the Browns came home from that first trip of the year with their rear ends dragging. A 28-10 loss to Philadelphia in the regular-season opener made it look as if 1954 would be a long year.

But they rebounded and beat the Chicago Cardinals at home and won eight of the next nine games and won the NFL title over Detroit, 56-10.

It was then that Otto Graham decided to retire, but he couldn't resist the $25,000 offered by the Browns and the pleas of his coach. So he came back and the Browns won another title.

# Rickey's Motel an Oasis in Northern California

TRAINING CAMP CAN BE pretty boring for veterans. That was particularly true when you had the same coach year after year and practically the same offense and defense.

Hall of Fame quarterback Otto Graham became so tired of it that he announced his retirement after the Browns' 1954 National Football League championship season. His retirement was conditional, however.

If things didn't go well in the exhibitions the following summer, he would return for one more season. The Browns lost four of five games, bringing Graham back for the last warmup. He led the club to another title in 1955.

There were more exhibitions in those days when the club had its summer camp at Hiram College in nearby Hiram. If your team won the championship the previous year you played seven, starting with the College All-Star Game in Chicago.

NFL teams played six exhibition games through 1960 and five until 1969, when the league returned to a six-game exhibition schedule through 1977. Camps usually were in session for eight weeks.

So Graham's and others' boredom was understandable.

From the late 1950s through the early '70s, however, relief for the Browns came through a trip to California to play the Los Angeles Rams and the San Francisco 49ers. For a time, the club spent most of the 10 days in Los Angeles. But wiser heads prevailed and it was determined that the cooler climate of Northern California would be better suited for training.

Other teams visiting West Coast clubs had stayed at a motel in Palo Alto called Rickey's with field work at Stanford University.

Upon arrival at Rickey's, the players were delighted to find twin swimming pools and plenty of nearby golf courses and tennis courts. They were even happier to discover that they were housed two to a cabin in a very secluded area. The coaches, front-office people and media stayed in a six-story building at the far end of the compound.

Bedchecks were taken then, as they are to this day, but they were almost completely ineffective because of the layout.

Former assistant coach Eddie Ulinski remembers the evening when he discovered a young lady in the room of a rookie. She dashed out the door as Ulinski opened it. Ulinski grabbed at her, only to be left with just a wig in his hand. The young man didn't survive the final cut, but not because of the incident. He was cut because of a lack of speed.

The sun was beginning to peek over a nearby mountain one dawn at Rickey's when owner Art Modell went for an early morning stroll. He discovered assistant coach weaving toward his room.

"You'd better hit the sack," Modell advised. The only reply was a thumb to nose.

Rickey's lively lounge, which was off limits to the players, was a nightly gathering place for the front office people and the media.

Entertainment was provided by a piano player, but the most fun came during his breaks. That's when Leo Murphy, the now-retired long-time trainer, took a turn at what he called "tickling the ivories."

It was on the beautiful Stanford courts that former assistant coach Fritz Heisler and this writer established themselves as the camp tennis champs.

San Francisco is a beautiful city with many attractions and only 30 minutes from Palo Alto. But sometimes a stay at Rickey's would pass without even a visit from the Browns except to play the game.

My late wife, Pat, heard so much about Rickey's that she decided to see for herself one summer. She rounded up a sitter for the five children and bought an airline ticket by frugally budgeting her grocery money.

She had been there two days when I was called from lunch to the telephone. It was my brother-in-law, who started out asking about the team.

"I know you didn't call to talk about the Browns," I said. "What's the matter?

"Sharon [my oldest daughter] broke her leg," he said. "It's a bad one and they have to do surgery."

My wife was on the next plane home.

# ON AND OFF
# THE FIELD

# Paul Brown,
# Legendary Coach, Dies

August 6, 1991

A VALID ARGUMENT CAN be made that Paul Brown was the top football coach ever in the game. He won at every level—high school, big-time college, the service and then in the professional ranks.

But Brown was more than just a coach. He was a student of the game who had much to do with making professional football the attraction it is today. He made coaching a full-time job for himself and all his assistants.

Others had to follow suit or fall behind. So they did the logical thing—they copied his methods, both as a coach and innovator.

Brown died yesterday morning at his home in Cincinnati from complications caused by pneumonia. He was 82.

Some of Brown's greatest success came at Massillon High School, then at Ohio State University, where he won a national championship. But he made his name with the Browns, which he built and then put into a championship game the first 10 years of the team's existence.

And when some were saying he was over the hill, he came back to form another fine franchise—the Cincinnati Bengals—five years after being fired in Cleveland.

Browns majority owner Art Modell, who shocked the football world by firing Brown in 1963, praised him for his football achievements.

"I look back and am amazed at what he did in the early going. So many things that have happened for the good of the game are the result of his vision. He was years ahead of the others," Modell said yesterday.

"Paul Brown didn't invent the game of football. He was just the first to take it seriously," declared *Sport Magazine* in a December 1986 story selecting Brown as one of 40 people who changed sports in America in the last four decades. The magazine portrayed Brown as an intense individual who made coaching a 24-hour-a-day job and forced other pro football teams to keep up with him.

Sid Gillman, Brown's coaching contemporary for many years in the NFL, told the magazine he always felt that "before Paul Brown pro football was a 'daisy chain.' He brought a system into pro football. He brought a practice routine. He broke down practice into individual areas. He had position coaches. He was an organizational genius. Before Paul Brown, coaches just rolled the ball out on the practice field."

Brown was also reputed to be the first to use intelligence tests to learn a player's potential, to use notebooks and classroom techniques extensively, to make complete film-clip statistical studies, to grade his players from films, to seclude his players the night before a game, to use offensive guards as play messengers, to develop passing patterns and to develop a system for scouting college players.

Brown was elected to the Pro Football Hall of Fame at Canton in 1967, his first year of eligibility, and presented many associates for their own Hall of Fame inductions at Canton. He coached or worked with 14 Hall of Famers: Doug Atkins, Jim Brown, Willie Davis, Weeb Ewbank, Len Ford, Frank Gatski, Otto Graham, Forrest Gregg, Lou Groza, Dante Lavelli, Mike McCormack, Marion Motley, Bill Willis and Bobby Mitchell.

He helped teach the game to Ewbank, Don Shula, Chuck Noll and Bill Walsh, all of whom either played or coached under him. Those four coached nine of the 20 Super Bowl winners through 1986.

His coaching record for all levels—361-133-16 for a .725 winning percentage—is rivaled by few.

Brown organized the Browns in the All-American Football Conference in 1946 and proceeded to build a dynasty.

The first player Brown signed was the quarterback, Graham, whom he called "the greatest player I ever coached."

After winning all four conference titles and compiling a 47-4-3 record, the Browns were accepted into the National Football League in 1950, accompanied by much disdain and derision.

The Browns gained instant respect by beating the defending champion Philadelpia Eagles, 35-10, in the '50 season opener. That set the stage for a 12-2 mark and a championship in Brown's first NFL test.

Brown's 17-year record in Cleveland was 165-68-9.

Brown, who held the titles of coach-general manager throughout his career in Cleveland, was fired from both positions by Modell Jan. 9, 1963, following a 7-6-1 season.

A clash of personalities between Brown and Modell and their differences over the handling of Jim Brown and the late Ernie Davis reportedly were the main reasons for the dismissal.

With the urge to get back into pro football, Brown met with former Ohio Gov. James A. Rhodes in 1965 and they agreed that the state could accommodate another pro team in Cincinnati. The Cincinnati Bengals' franchise was launched in 1968 with founder Brown also the team's part owner, general manager and coach. By 1970, the Bengals were American Football Conference Central Division champions.

Brown coached the Bengals to an eight-year record of 55-56-1, highlighted by another division crown in 1975, his final year on the field.

Brown was born in Norwalk Sept. 7, 1908, but his family moved to Massillon when he was 9. It was in Massillon as a youngster and later as a high school player that his interest in football and love of the game began and were nurtured.

After coaching at Severn Prep in Maryland, he returned home

and achieved nationwide acclaim by leading the Massillon High Tigers to an 80-8-2 record from 1932-40. Massillon's stadium was named "Paul Brown Tiger Stadium" in his honor in 1976.

At Ohio State University, his teams of 1941-43 were 18-8-1, which included a national championship in 1942.

Brown's oldest son, Robin, died of cancer in 1977. Brown's first wife, Katy, died in April 1969. He remarried in June 1973. His wife, Mary, was a widow with four children at the time.

His son Mike is the Bengals' assistant general manager, and his youngest son, Pete, is director.

Brown authored a book—*PB: The Paul Brown Story*—with writer Jack Clary in 1976. He concluded it with the word of Dean Elizabeth Hamilton of Miami University, where he attended college.

"The eternal verities will always prevail. Such things as truth, honesty, character and loyalty will never change." And Brown added, "I have tried to live my whole life by those words—and it has made me a happy man."

# Brown Remembered as Pioneer, Innovator

August 6, 1991

ART MODELL, THE MAN who fired Paul Brown as general manager and coach of the Browns in January 1963, said yesterday he was saddened by the death of the football giant.

"Despite our differences I regarded him as a man who was great for professional football," Modell said. "He was an innovator and a pioneer in the game.

"I look back and am amazed at what he did in the early going. So many things that have happened for the good of the game are the result of his vision. He was years ahead of the others.

"He even won in service football."

Brown was fired after a 7-6-1 season in 1962, but that record was not the reason for the dismissal. It was a personality clash of two strong-willed men and Brown could not reconcile himself to a hands-on owner after directing every aspect of the club from its inception in 1946.

The breakup was characterized by bitter feelings for years, but the passage of time mellowed both men. They never became close friends, but they got back together to some extent at NFL meetings and social gatherings at those huddles.

"We got closer some years back," Modell said. "We never became bosom buddies to the point of playing gin rummy together on Saturday nights, but we did get closer.

"Paul was a conservative and I lean that way sometimes. So we were on the same side of the fence at many NFL meetings.

"We were on the same side on the merger of the AFL and the

NFL alignment. We got, I believe, a new respect for each other with the passage of time."

Modell recalled that he was instrumental in bringing Brown back into football through the franchise granted to the Cincinnati Bengals. He OK'd placing another pro team in the state.

"I worked with Gov. Jim Rhodes on this," Modell said. "If it wasn't for me I don't believe he would have been back in the game. And the rivalry with the Bengals has become a very good one.

"This has been one of my proudest achievements."

As soon as he was informed of Brown's death, Modell ordered his staff to have a moment of silence in memory of Brown at last night's exhibition game between the Browns and the Tampa Bay Buccaneers.

Many other NFL owners, coaches and players expressed similar sentiments when they learned of Brown's death. Accolades swept in from all parts of the nation.

Lin Houston and Tommy James, both of whom played for Brown at Massillon, Ohio State and the Browns, were about to tee off at Brookside Country Club in Canton when they received the news.

"I wouldn't have played for him at all those places if I didn't like and respect him," said James, a defensive back. "We had a few differences, but he treated me just fine. He always told us football was secondary to an education."

Houston, who spent part of his years with the Browns as a "messenger guard," running in plays, said, "I know that nobody lives forever, but this was a real loss.

"I spent 13 years under Paul. I regard him as a super coach. He taught a lot of coaches how this game is played."

Fellow Hall of Famer Tom Landry, former coach of the Dallas Cowboys, said that Brown "pretty much shaped my coaching philosophy. No one had more influence on me than he had. He was the first IBM coach. He used the briefcase and the hat.

"He brought organization into pro football. We thought we had to perfect our defense to the point they perfected their offense."

When Lou Groza, who had spent a year at Ohio State, came out of the U.S. Army in World War II, Brown signed him as a place-kicker and offensive tackle. Known as the Toe, Groza is in the Hall of Fame.

"We had a good relationship," said Groza, now an insurance executive. "When I had a problem I could go directly to him. He always has kept track of his former players. Paul was a tough disciplinarian and a fine organizer and got good players and good assistant coaches."

Brown used to describe Mike McCormack as "the finest offensive lineman I ever coached." McCormack had an equally high opinion of the coach.

"We've lost a real giant of the game," he said. "He was such a great innovator and at his best when the game was kind of teetering.

"Remember how he was severely criticized for calling the plays? Now there isn't a level of football in which the coach doesn't do this."

McCormack said he last saw Brown at the NFL meetings in Hawaii in March. "We had what must have been a 40-minute talk," he said. "I'm so glad for that."

Miami coach Don Shula played for Brown and as a player at John Carroll spent much time watching Brown's teams.

"With the passing of Paul Brown, football has lost one of the great contributors to the game," Shula said. "I feel privileged to have played for him and to have worked for him for over 15 years on the league competition committee. He had a profound impact on my development as a coach."

Former Browns and Cincinnati coach Forrest Gregg remembered that Brown gave him a second opportunity to coach in the NFL. "I will never forget that and will always appreciate that," Gregg, now athletic director at Southern Methodist, said. "I really respected the man. He had a wonderful eye for talent."

Marion Motley, Browns fullback, 1946 to 1953—"He was such an innovator. You know, he came up with the split end, and he was the first to move the halfbacks around so that the defense had to move with them. Everyone else just followed him."

Taylor Smith, president of the Atlanta Falcons—"He and George Halas [late founder of the Chicago Bears] were like the fathers of the NFL. He is one of the true greats of all time in the history of the NFL."

Michael R. White, Cleveland mayor—"The game of football has lost one of its giants. Paul Brown, probably more so than any other individual, is responsible for transforming the game of football into the popular national sport that we enjoy today. He was an innovator, a competitor unlike any other the sport has seen. Because of his special significance to Cleveland, I urge all residents to join me in extending condolences to his family and friends."

John Wooten, Browns lineman, 1959-1967—"He was such an outstanding technician. With that I mean the head, the feet, the steps. His game and his knowledge of the game was unbelievable. He was so far ahead as far as teaching and the fundamentals of the game. Other people were working just during the season. He was working all year round."

Bill (Tiger) Johnson, former Bengals head and assistant coach—"It's not a happy day and it is difficult for me. The things I remember most are when I was with the 49ers as a player and coach. The Browns were always our biggest rival and I always placed Paul above everyone. He was untouchable, an idol, in a position of reverence. He was all those years bigger than life. And none of that changed years later when I went to work for him. He was forever a leader in our profession."

Weeb Ewbank, former New York Jets and Baltimore Colts head coach, an assistant with Brown at Great Lakes and at Cleveland— "This is very hard for me. Our families were so close. My wife, Lucy, and his [first] wife, Katie, often took long walks together. I meant to call him last week but could not get through. Paul was to be my presenter at the Pro Football Hall of Fame, but that was the year his son, Robin, died [1978]. He was one of the greatest as a man and a coach. He was a gentleman and a wonderful friend."

John Pont, longtime college coach and a charter member of Miami University's "Cradle of Coaches" like Brown—"He was a good friend. I know a great deal will be said of his football and innovative contributions and what he did for and with his players. When I first started coaching in 1956, I went to the Browns' camp in Hiram, Ohio. I was a rookie coach, but he was one of the most gracious and courteous individuals I ever met. He always had a kind word and a smile. He was a gentleman in every sense of the word. He had very strong convictions and, throughout his life, he did not change them."

Gerry Faust, former coach at Cincinnati Moeller High School, Notre Dame and now coach at University of Akron—"He and his wife Mary treated me first class when I was a high-school coach even though he had no reason to do that. He was a great man and I will miss him."

Jack Clary, Brown's official biographer—"Personally, I am saddened. I lost a dear friend, the finest person next to my father I have ever known. He was a wise and compassionate man. The game itself should be saddened. He was probably the wisest man in the game today who is responsible for the game reaching the heights it has."

Boomer Esiason, Bengals quarterback—"When I was a rookie, I got a chance to sit next to him on the bus on the way to a game. He said to me, 'Boomer, don't ever forget the people who came before you and made football the game it is today.'"

# Paul Brown Gave and Expected Loyalty

PAUL BROWN WAS LIKE most of us, something of a paradox. He could be as sentimental as a man looking back at his first prom and hard-nosed as a banker making a foreclosure.

Loyalty was the attribute he treasured most. He gave it and he expected it in return. A breach of it by one he had considered a friend never was forgotten.

Like most successful persons in business or sports, he had a large ego. He was a very interesting man to be around.

Brown was not an extrovert. He seemed almost shy at times. But he did an excellent job in front of a microphone. And no coach ever handled the postgame interviews with more aplomb no matter what the outcome.

An octogenerian piles up a heap of memories. Brown was no exception and perhaps more than most enjoyed reminiscing. Old friends, who passed his test of loyalty over the decades, always had a warm place in his heart.

He often spoke of Dave Stewart, his high school football coach at Massillon who was a major influence. He remained close to players such as Lin Houston and Tommy James, who played for him in high school, college and with the Browns.

As a general manager, he negotiated contracts. This didn't endear him to the players any more than his strictness as a coach, but later they became "my boys." Lou Groza, Otto Graham, Dante Lavelli, Bill Willis, Marion Motley and most of the others became big Paul Brown boosters and friends as the decades rolled along.

Brown's friendship with former coaches Dick Gallagher, Weeb Ewbank, Fritz Heisler, Howard Brinker, Eddie Ulinski and scores of others never wavered. And he had a very close relationship with some of the media, particularly Luther Emory of the *Massillon Independent* and Paul Hornung of the *Columbus Dispatch*.

The late Blanton Collier was one of his closest confidants for a long time. They met at Great Lakes Naval Station and coached together with the Browns. The friendship ended abruptly when Collier took the reins of the Browns after Brown was fired by Art Modell on the first Monday of 1963.

If Brown had a hint that he would be dismissed, he did a good job of keeping it a secret a few nights before on New Year's Eve. My wife and I saw the New Year in with him, his first wife, Katie, and son, Mike, at Shaker Country Club. There were rumors that things weren't going well between him and Modell, but few anticipated the complete severing of their relationship. Brown seemed at peace with the world that night.

Through many years of Browns' watching for the *Plain Dealer*, some vignettes of Brown are particularly vivid.

As the father of three boys, he enjoyed seeing daughters of the media and his coaches at the Hiram College training camp. The door of his room usually would be open and my daughters, Sharon and Allie, frequently would venture inside. They knew there always was a box of chocolates in the dresser drawer.

Daily sessions with the media were informal. Brown would climb the hill from practice at Hiram, kick off his shoes and socks, cool his feet on the tile floor, take a seat on the bed and answer any questions.

He often enjoyed a scotch and water before dinner, but asked his players to abstain during the training season. He did the same even on his birthday.

There was one such anniversary when the team was in Dallas for an exhibition and several of the writers toasted him with champagne. Brown replied with soda water. "I can't do what I ask the players not to do," he said.

Brown aged slowly and gracefully, but during the days at Hiram it was noted that he needed longer arms if he was to continue reading his morning *Plain Dealer*. He finally got some bifocals, but wore them sparingly.

Jim Brown was one player he never seemed able to understand or relate to. It was an uneasy relationship through their six years together although they later became friends and were partners in golf matches.

Brown lived well during his "exile" in La Jolla, Calif., after having been fired by the Browns. Looking out the kitchen window at San Diego Bay, it was suggested that he couldn't have it better, $82,500 a year for not coaching.

"Oh, I'll be back," he said. And he was a few years later after founding the Cincinnati Bengals.

Katie died in 1968, the year Brown moved back into football with the Bengals. It had been a loving marriage and the tears flowed freely from the usually stoic Brown as he walked away from her gravesite in Massillon.

Brown enjoyed good health through most of his long lifetime. It wasn't until the last year and a half that it began to deteriorate. He rallied from some breathing problems last spring to fly to Hawaii to attend NFL meetings.

He had some advice for Don Weiss, the league's executive director, as the huddle concluded.

"Never become an octogenerian," he said with a smile.

# Trading Bobby Mitchell

THE BROWNS SHIPPED RUNNING back Bobby Mitchell to the Redskins in 1961. He turned out to be a Hall of Fame wide receiver. The Browns didn't even get much in the deal. The trade widened the gap between Browns owner Art Modell and coach Paul Brown. Brown was fired after the 1962 season.

Brown made the swap with Washington owner George Preston Marshall during the 1961 season, but it went into effect at the end of the season. Modell was not consulted about trading Mitchell, a swift halfback who complemented the skills of Jim Brown as an outside threat.

The Browns were playing in Dallas on Dec. 3, 1961, when the rumor spread that Mitchell was going to the Redskins.

I checked with Modell right after Cleveland's 38-17 victory over the Cowboys.

"It's true," Modell said. "Marshall called me and asked me what I thought of the deal. That's the first I had heard about it. Then he started kidding me about not knowing what was going on with my own team."

Modell said this week he was pretty steamed by the needling by Marshall. The late Redskins owner finally had decided he would integrate the Redskins, the last all-white club in the National Football League.

Brown knew Mitchell was a quality performer, but he was intrigued by the idea of having two big backs together in his offense. He saw the success that the combination of Jim Taylor and Paul Hornung was bringing to Green Bay.

Instead of returning home on the Cleveland charter from Dallas, we (Modell, Brown and the media) flew to Chicago for the Monday draft meeting. It was held in the Chicago Sheraton Hotel.

That was the last draft, as I recall, where the teams all sat in one room and did their selecting. Not far from the meeting room was the Goliwog Room, a popular watering spot.

The draft was held early, with two games remaining in the season, because the American Football League was competing for the collegiate talent.

The Redskins, with the worst record in the league at the time, had the first pick and selected Ernie Davis, a king-sized running back from Syracuse.

Brown used his first selection to get Gary Collins, a wide receiver from Maryland who was to later become the most valuable player in the Browns' 1964 NFL championship victory over Baltimore.

Cleveland had a second pick in that first round and chose Leroy Jackson, a running back from Western Illinois. Mitchell and Jackson were sent to Washington for the rights to Davis. It was only the NFL rights, however, as Buffalo of the AFL, had also selected Davis.

Mitchell was serving in the National Guard at Fort Meade, Md., during the week and joined the Browns on weekends. Now assistant general manager with the Redskins, he recalled last week how he first had a hint that something was up. "I was lined up for reveille at about 5 a.m. when one of the Washington players also in the Guard asked me if I'd heard about the big trade," Mitchell said. "I didn't realize I was involved.

"I wasn't home to read the Cleveland newspapers. I did suspect something was up when I was held out of the last game of the season, a tie with the Giants in New York. I think we might have won that game if I played."

Mitchell recalled that Brown came over to him in the locker room at Yankee Stadium after the game.

"He sort of said goodbye, but never said that I was going to Washington," Mitchell said. "I think I finally heard it from Jim Brown who said he had nothing to do with my leaving. And I don't think he did."

Mitchell said it was a blow to learn that he and several other black players were selected to integrate the Redskins. "I loved it in Cleveland and had just bought a house there," he said. "And in those days no one wanted to go to the Redskins, particularly from a winning team like the Browns."

Mitchell said the move was "traumatic."

"I was buffeted on all sides after I got there," he said. "Some of the white people resented me being on the team. I couldn't do enough to please the blacks.

"But it has all turned out wonderfully. I surely then never thought I'd still be here some 20 years later."

Asked by Brown, Modell agreed to take on the job of signing Collins and Davis. The late Paul Bixler, then the team's personnel man, and Modell flew to Maryland and got Collins to agree.

They got a scare flying through thick fog in a small prop plane to Elmira, N.Y., to sign Davis. Buffalo made a strong bid, but Modell and Bixler persuaded Davis to join the Browns and team with Jim Brown, another Syracuse graduate.

Davis complained of a sore throat when he stopped at the Browns training camp at Hiram College en route to the college All-Star game in Chicago the next July. A few days later I had a call waiting when I arrived at the Palmer House Hotel in Chicago. Modell asked me to come to his room right away.

The late Frank Gibbons of the old *Cleveland Press* was there and Modell seemed very upset.

"I have very bad news," he said. "Ernie [Davis] has leukemia but he hasn't been told. Please just say he is ill and can't play for a while."

Davis did go through a remission from the disease and wanted to play. Modell agreed, but Brown thought it was best that he didn't. His No. 45 is retired, but Davis never played a down for the Browns before he died the following spring after standing on the sideline for most of the Browns practices in 1962.

The breach between Modell and Brown widened during that

7-6-1 season. Brown was fired in January 1963 and a new era in Cleveland's pro football history began.

Bill McPeak, the late coach of the Redskins, quickly switched Mitchell to wide receiver. It was his success at that position that put him in the Hall of Fame.

# Sipe's Legacy Likely Will Be Red Right 88

THIS WRITER DOESN'T PRETEND to have the eye for football talent of an Ernie Accorsi, a Mike Lombardi or a Bill Belichick. But back in 1972, I did guess right on a handsome young quarterback named Brian Sipe.

Sipe was a 13th-round draft pick who had come to Cleveland with the other draftees and free agents for a March minicamp. The weather was typical for March in Cleveland—miserable—so coach Nick Skorich gathered the hopefuls in the Exhibition Hall of Public Hall.

The large pillars and low ceiling made it difficult to tell much about passers or receivers. So it was mostly an interview with the young man from San Diego State that impressed me.

After talking to Sipe, I wrote that he "very well might be the team's quarterback of the future." It wasn't anticipated, I admit, that a decade later he would be at the top of the National Football League's ladder of quarterbacks, voted MVP of the league for 1980.

I didn't foresee, either, that he was going to forever be connected to one play—Red Right 88. That was the pass intended for tight end Ozzie Newsome in the playoff game against the Oakland Raiders on Jan. 4, 1981.

Trailing, 14-12, the Browns were within field-goal range for Don Cockroft. But it was a nasty day with a swirling wind and frozen field at the Stadium. So on third down, coach Sam Rutigliano opted to try for a touchdown with a pass.

Few Browns fans have forgotten what happened on Red Right 88. Sipe's pass wobbled into the hands of defensive back Mike

Davis, and the Raiders went on to win that game and the Super Bowl.

Sipe says the play doesn't haunt him.

"I didn't dwell on it until it consumed me," he said. "It was an icy field and a windy day. The play was called for me, not by me.

"It was a bad pass. I probably shouldn't have attempted it because of the coverage."

A few weeks after that play, I was with Sipe in New York City, where he received the Pro Football Writers MVP award. It was his first trip to the area, except for a game.

He walked the streets in anonymity, but once he entered the Torch Room at Gallagher's Restaurant to receive the award, the same question came from all the news media representatives there: "What happened on that last play?"

Sipe later told me that he guessed it was something he would have to live with the whole off-season.

"It's really a shame," he said at the time. "I hope the fans, particularly in Cleveland, won't forget it was a good season and the future looks so good.

"I'm not going to apologize for the interception, and I'm not trying to dodge the responsibility for it. We got there by taking chances. It got us a long way. It is unfortunate so many remember just the interception."

Rutigliano put his arm around Sipe when the quarterback came off the field after the pass. But the two were not as close as they might have seemed then.

Sipe had special feelings for Skorich, the coach who kept him with the team through two years on the reserve squad.

"When I came back after my first season, they had picked up a quarterback named Don Horn to be the backup passer [to Mike Phipps]," Sipe said. "But Nick told me I could do the job in the NFL. And he kept me around for another year."

Sipe also had high regard for Jim Shofner and Blanton Collier. Both were his quarterback coaches in Cleveland at various times.

"It's a lonely job, being a quarterback," Sipe said. "Coming off the field and having someone like Jim Shofner to talk to was great. And Blanton knew so much about the game and the position, he had a profound effect on me mentally."

Sipe, who left the Browns for the New Jersey Generals of the United States Football League, became friendly again with Peter Hadhazy then. But it took a little forgiving after an incident in Denver in 1976, when the Browns lost, 44-13.

Hadhazy, a vice president with the power of general manager, came into the dressing room at Mile High Stadium after the defeat. Sipe heard his name used and saw the news media around Hadhazy. It wasn't until he read the *Plain Dealer* the next morning that he learned the boss had said Sipe "never would be an NFL quarterback."

Hadhazy never really apologized for the incident, which drew big headlines, but he did hint to Sipe that he wished he hadn't made the remarks. Later, they became friends in the USFL, where Hadhazy was second in command of the league.

Sipe left the Browns after the 1983 season, when the team went 9-7 but failed to make the playoffs.

He went to the USFL for several reasons. He said he thought Paul McDonald was the quarterback Rutigliano wanted to run the team. He also received a big financial package that was guaranteed.

He said he has had no regrets.

"I sensed that I needed a change," he said. "And maybe the team did, too."

Sipe often carried a large book on the road and perused it on airplanes. I thought at first that it might be a Bible, but later discovered that they mostly were about architecture.

"I always have been interested in architecture, but was persuaded to go to San Diego State, where they didn't have a major in it," he said. "But I read about it and often spent my time on the road looking at various buildings in the cities we visited."

It all helped.

Now he and his family—wife Jeri and their three children—are living in the same manner they became accustomed to in football. Sipe is using that architectural interest with Wavecrest, which builds luxury homes in the San Diego area.

Sipe said his favorite structure is Cleveland Stadium.

"I got goose bumps when I first saw it," he said. "I just stood there staring at it the first day I came to Cleveland. That's the kind of a place where football should be played and where I wanted to play. I hope the Browns never move from there."

# Publicist Knew How to Find the Beef

IT WAS DRAFT DAY at the Browns headquarters more than a few years back and an enterprising reporter covering the beat saw team publicist Nate Wallack scribbling notes on a sheet of paper. Sensing an exclusive story, the sports writer took a peek and read four CBs, three RBs, and four LBs.

A scoop is a scoop no matter how attained, so the writer called his office. "The Browns are going to draft four cornerbacks, three running backs and four linebackers," he told the rewrite man.

But as it turned out, Wallack was merely making out the luncheon list for some of the coaches in the draft room—four corned beef sandwiches, three roast beefs and four lox on bagels.

Wallack, who died on Jan. 16, 1984, loved to tell that story with a chuckle. The rotund vice president of publicity also served a stretch in the same capacity with the Indians. In both jobs, he enjoyed good food and fine restaurants almost as much as he liked his work and the people he was involved with each day.

I will always think of Nate when I go to Cincinnati, one of my favorite cities to visit.

Wallack was fond of Cincinnati, also. I know he liked the idea that it has a bustling downtown, which is now filled with new hotels.

But even more importantly, it has excellent restaurants. And there is none better in the state, and maybe in the nation, than the Maisonette.

For many years, Wallack traveled in advance of the team when the Browns played out of town. His primary mission was to deliver film clips to the TV stations and news reports to radio people and sports writers.

But he always found time to scout the restaurants and pick his favorite as a place to entertain the media and front office personnel on Saturday nights. And he never found a bad one, not even Chili John's in Green Bay.

Sometimes even the coach would forget the Xs and Os for a few hours and join in these off-the-record huddles. Writers got to test their taste buds with a variety of foods. One visiting journalist even ordered chateaubriand for two in Toots Shor's eatery in Manhattan.

Like a good maitre d', Wallack would go from table to table or around a big table on some occasions to make sure everybody was enjoying the repast. Often, he would sample the various dishes.

But Wallack was more than a gourmet. He was a kindly man with a heart as big as his tummy.

When one veteran writer died a long time ago, Nate learned that the widow and children were left with some heavy debts. He quickly but quietly tapped sports moguls in the area and raised the funds with no fanfare.

There was an occasion when I missed a trip to New Orleans with the Browns because of an illness. Wallack called to see how I was doing.

"I've just been to the cathedral here and lighted a candle for you," this man of the Jewish faith said to his Catholic friend.

Wallack's card-playing buddies on these trips remember him well, usually to their financial sorrow. The night before he died, he spent much of the evening playing uno with TV sportscaster Gib Shanley.

Those who sat down for gin rummy with him on the road knew when he really meant business. He would interrupt the game long enough to strip down to his shorts, then continue in earnest.

Wallack, as the years piled up, used to enjoy reminiscing about his early days. To earn extra money as a youth, he was a sandlot baseball and amateur basketball scorer. Later, as a social worker at the Warrensville Workhouse, he established the first Alcoholics Anonymous group there and was proud of this accomplishment.

He also was the publicist for the Cleveland team in the National Basketball League, and for the Cleveland Rams before they moved to Los Angeles. He remained in Cleveland to join the newly organized Browns. During his early days with the Browns, the team flew DC-3 planes. He remembered how he would distribute the players according to weight to keep the plane on level.

His wife, Ruth, and their sons—Stuart and Lewis—came first in his life. He also used to say that he had his own sports hall of fame and that it had tougher requirements than the shrines for football and baseball. The only two members were Al Lopez, former manager of the Indians, and Art Modell, his boss and good friend with the Browns.

Hal Lebovitz, longtime sports editor for the *Plain Dealer*, was his best friend in the media. They talked every day, sometimes twice a day.

Some of the Browns' entourage still dine at the Maisonette. If they do, I hope they pause for just a moment before starting on the pheasant under glass or some such delicacy and lift a toast to Uncle Nate, as he often was called.

He would have liked that.

# Talent, Grit Made Graham the Best

CHAMPIONSHIP FOOTBALL TEAMS USUALLY have very good quarterbacks. Otto Graham, who won seven championships and played in 10 league title games in his 10 years with the Browns, might be the best of all time at his position.

Next on my ranking of the Browns passers are Bernie Kosar and Brian Sipe, ranked about even. They had different styles, but both got the most out of their teams.

Graham was a better all-round athlete than Kosar or Sipe. He was mostly a pocket passer, but also was an effective running threat.

A tailback at Northwestern, Graham played a year of professional basketball.

Graham received some injuries, but none so bad that he couldn't start the next game. The most publicized injury came in 1953 against the San Francisco 49ers, when Graham was pushed out of bounds by defensive back Fred Bruney and then hit in the face by linebacker Art Michalik.

Dr. Vic Ippolito the club's longtime doctor, remembered the incident.

"The cut must have required almost 20 stitches," he said. "The teeth were jammed back against the tonsil area. I put the stitches in with someone holding a flashlight for me."

The other Browns were already on the field for the second half when Ippolito finished treating Graham.

"I said, 'Let's go out' to Otto, but didn't think about him playing," Ippolito said. "By the time I got to the bench, he was on the field."

Coach Paul Brown had equipment manager Morrie Kono attach an inch-thick piece of clear plastic to Graham's helmet.

Graham proceeded to complete 9 of 10 passes in the second half and the Browns won, 23-21.

It was at the end of that season that Brown began working on a protective device that eventually became the facemask.

That wasn't the first game Graham showed his courage. In 1948, when the Browns were in the All-America Conference, they had to play three games in eight days. They played in New York on Nov. 21, at Los Angeles on Nov. 25, and at San Francisco on Nov. 28.

The Browns beat Los Angeles, 31-14, but Graham suffered stretched ligaments in his right knee when he was hit while trying to pass. He could barely walk after the game.

Graham tested the leg before the kickoff in San Francisco and found he could hand off the ball and get back into the pocket. So Brown started him. Graham quickly got a chance to play when the 49ers fumbled on their first play.

Behind great protection, Graham passed to Dante Lavelli for a touchdown. The Browns fell behind, 21-10, in the second half, but rallied to win, 31-28, with Graham throwing three more touchdown passes.

Graham was the quarterback for the Browns' first 10 seasons and the team has had good luck with starting quarterbacks since. There was, however, a down time after Graham retired following the 1955 campaign. A variety of quarterbacks were used, starting with George Ratterman, a former Notre Dame player.

Milt Plum came in from Penn State in 1957 and shared the job with Tommy O'Connell and John Borton as the club won the Eastern Conference title. Jim Ninowski was drafted the next year, but went to Detroit and returned when Plum was swapped to the Lions.

Frank Ryan came to the club in 1962 and got his chance when an injury put Ninowski on the sideline. Ryan engineered Cleveland's last NFL title in 1964.

When Bill Nelsen arrived from Pittsburgh in a trade in 1968, I didn't think he had a chance of unseating Ryan. But he did and had five pretty good seasons in Cleveland despite the gimpiest knees of anyone who ever played the position in Cleveland.

Because of those knees, owner Art Modell continued to search for help at the position. He thought he had it when the trade that sent wide receiver Paul Warfield to the Miami Dolphins brought in Mike Phipps with a No. 1 draft pick in 1970.

Phipps looked like the answer on paper, but the chemistry wasn't there. When he went down with an injury in 1975, Sipe took over.

The Browns had some great days under Sipe, including the Kardiac Kids years. But he went off to the World Football League after the 1983 season. After Paul McDonald had a rough season in 1984, Kosar was drafted in the 1985 supplemental draft.

# Sense of Humor
# Served Modell Well

WHEN I FIRST MET Art Modell in Miami on Jan. 7, 1961, neither of us probably thought our relationship would last for more than three decades.

In 1961 there was a story in the *Plain Dealer* from Miami, where the Browns were playing the Detroit Lions in the Playoff Bowl, that Modell, a 35-year old New York television and advertising executive, headed a group about to purchase the team. At halftime of the game, a friend took me across the Orange Bowl field to meet him.

Modell was seated with Browns President Dave Jones and treasurer Bob Gries. Modell said he had been ducking reporters because he thought all statements should come from the present owners.

"We had hoped this story wouldn't break until after today's game," he said. "Once everything has been worked out, I will be glad to talk to anybody."

The Browns lost to the Lions, 17-16. Final details of the sale were put together and all the papers were signed in Cleveland.

Modell quickly sat down for an interview with me in his suite in the Sheraton Cleveland Hotel. After purchasing the Browns, Modell and some partners owned the hotel briefly in the 1970s.

Modell had dinner with Browns offensive tackle and placekicker Lou Groza the night before we talked.

"I surprised him by naming eight of the players on the Browns' 1946 team from the old All-America Conference," Modell said.

A short time later, Modell was out holding the football in Berea for Groza's kicks. He persuaded the veteran, who had retired after the 1959 season, to return and Groza had seven more successful seasons as a place-kicker.

As Browns beat writer and a columnist for the *Plain Dealer*, I have seen a great deal of Modell since he bought the team. He always has been an activist owner and an excellent spokesman for his team.

Some small vignettes about Modell stick out in my memory.

Modell always will be remembered as the man who fired Hall of Fame coach Paul Brown. It came on a January day in 1963 when the Cleveland daily newspapers were on strike.

I was working for WJW-TV Channel 8 during that lull and was sent to the Stadium with a cameraman to interview Modell. I remember asking him if he was changing the name of the Browns to "the Modells."

He appeared a bit startled for a few seconds. Then that sense of humor took over and he just laughed as he said, "No."

I remember him at Doctor's Hospital in New York City in May 1969. He was suffering from a bleeding stomach ulcer, but that didn't stop him from looking after the team's business. At that time he was agreeing to move the club into the American Football Conference. Pittsburgh's Art Rooney and his son, Dan, had just left the room after agreeing to switch their team to the AFC. New York Giants President Wellington Mara, who gave his blessing for the move, also had departed just before my telephone call.

"Dan [Rooney] didn't want to move but his dad said 'I'm going along with Art,' and the impasse was broken," Modell said.

That same year, he was married in Las Vegas to Pat Breslin, a television actress who had roots in New York City. She quickly found the Browns and media would be a major part of her life.

While still on their honeymoon, the Modells joined the team for exhibition games in Los Angeles and San Diego. They spent almost a week at a waterfront hotel in San Diego with the Browns' front office folks and writers, TV people and many of their wives.

That same week, the group met activist Angela Davis, the sister of cornerback Ben Davis.

A social being, Modell introduced the practice of taking his front office people and the media to dinner the night before road games. Nate Wallack, the team's publicist, enjoyed food and picked out the best-known eateries for the dinners. These restaurants included the Maisonette in Cincinnati, Toot Shor's in New York, the Green House in Kansas City, Mateo's in Los Angeles, the London Chop House in Detroit, the Red Carpet in Chicago, the Columbia in Tampa, Fla., Duke Ziebert's in Washington, D.C., Commander's Palace in New Orleans and many others. No wonder members of the media always had to go on diets after the season.

During one NFL meeting at the Palm Canyon Hotel and Resort in Palm Springs, Calif., Modell introduced the group to margaritas after an afternoon of tennis. It was a delightful alcoholic concoction served in miniature fish bowls. I've never been able to make them taste as good at home.

There have been downs as well as ups. Arguments of some violence have taken place between us, but most were soon forgotten with a few laughs. There has been much more fun than fights. The memories are mostly good.

# Brown Had Winning Look on Sideline

BACK IN THE DAYS when the *Plain Dealer* paid reporters to speak to groups in the area, I used to go out regularly. And most of the time I got a few laughs with a story about the late Paul Brown.

The story went something like this: A Browns fan died and went to heaven and discovered a football game going on. There was a man on the sideline in a camel hair coat and snap brim felt hat coaching one team. "That looks like Paul Brown," the fan said to the angel seated next to him. "No, that's not Paul Brown," said the angel. "It's just God pretending he's Paul Brown."

The brown suit, shirt and tie, either a straw or felt hat and camel hair overcoat in cooler weather were Brown's trademarks.

In fact, that type of attire was pretty much generally worn when Brown, who died in 1991, broke into the pro game in 1946. Jim Lee Howell, a former coach of the New York Giants, always dressed that way.

So did Vince Lombardi on cold afternoons in Green Bay, Wis., and Tom Landry on the Dallas sidelines.

I remember when Sam Rutigliano and I were discussing famous coaches as models for others in the business.

"Don't tell Art [Modell, Browns president] that I told you this, but Paul Brown was the coach I admired most as a young man in the business," Rutigliano said. "I'd go to a Giants game and see him on the sideline with the Browns. The way he dressed, the way he acted, you just knew that he was good at what he was doing.

"I always wanted to look like he did on the sideline."

Most of the truly good coaches I've known were disciplined people in their coaching and private lives. Brown had a routine he followed throughout his career as coach and general manager.

His practices were not lengthy, usually an hour and a half, and he always quit exactly on time. When he coached the Browns, he would get home for dinner every night and often took a walk in his Shaker Heights neighborhood. Many of his neighbors became his good friends.

He enjoyed having a scotch and water before dinner, but just one. And when he asked the players not to drink or smoke during training camp, he also abstained.

On his birthday in 1954, the Browns were playing Detroit in an exhibition game in Dallas. The late Russ Gestner, former Browns business manager, bought a few bottles of champagne and invited the media and Brown to a celebration. Brown was relaxed and friendly, but settled for some ginger ale.

It might have been the regularity of his habits that helped him maintain such good health for the most part. During the time I covered the Browns, I recall him not feeling well only twice.

Once, he missed part of a practice to have some dental work done. The other time, he had the flu. But he drove his car close to the practice field at League Park and opened and closed the window to send in plays.

During his days in La Jolla, Calif., after he was fired by the Browns, many friends visited him and his wife, Katy. He seemed to enjoy being the host and loved to point out the beauties of the San Diego Bay, which could be seen from the kitchen of their condominium.

During one visit, I came down with a virus and left for Cleveland not feeling well. I appreciated his call that night to see if I had made it home all right and was feeling better.

He maintained that home in San Diego as a winter spot after taking over the Bengals. My wife, Cece, and I visited during the Super Bowl in San Diego and we went to his golf club for dinner.

Service was slow and we all, including Brown, had several alcoholic drinks. As we waited for the car to be brought around to take us home, he handed the car keys over to Mary, whom he married some years after Katy's death.

"Wouldn't some of my players love to see the headline 'P.B. Arrested on DWI Charge'," he said with a chuckle.

It didn't seem the same not to have him at Wilmington College, where the Bengals hold training camp, the last two years. Wearing a large straw plantation-style hat, he used to be on the sideline at every practice.

He was ill in the summer of 1991 when I visited Wilmington and he died a short time later. The camp seemed to run smoothly last summer, but it was strange without Brown.

After he retired from coaching after the 1975 season, he always sat in a loge next to the press box at home games. There were probably two dozen people in the loge with him, but his complete concentration was on the action.

# On the Trail of a Coaching Change in '77

THE LATE PAUL BROWN used to have an almost daily morning greeting when he saw reporters at breakfast at the Hiram College training camp.

"Well, do you have a scoop today?" he would ask as he opened his morning *Plain Dealer*.

Brown was kidding, of course. But those were the days of *Plain Dealer* rivalry with the old *Cleveland News* and *Press* and an exclusive story did pop up now and then.

I had my share of them over the years, but the stretch I remember best came in December 1977. I really was on a roll with three "scoops" in three days.

The first of those was on the departure of Forrest Gregg as coach of the Browns. The same story said that defensive coordinator Dick Modzelewski would be interim coach for the last game of the season in Seattle. And the third was the first mention in Cleveland that Sam Rutigliano would be the new coach.

The headline across the top of the *Plain Dealer* sports page on Dec. 13 read "Browns Coach Gregg To Quit."

After a 5-2 start, the Browns had lost five of their last six, a slump started by Cincinnati at the Stadium. There had been rumors that club President Art Modell was becoming disenchanted with his coach.

Then I received a tip on Gregg's departure from a person very close to the team at a Christmas cocktail party the night before a 19-15 loss to the Houston Oilers, also on the lakefront. (Actually, my wife, Cece, was instrumental in the whole affair, after talking with Art Modell's wife, Pat.)

On Monday I made some telephone calls and became 99 percent sure that the firing or resignation was about to happen. I called Gregg at his Berea office. Dick Evans, a coaching aide, answered the phone and said Gregg was tied up.

"Tell him he's about to be relieved of his duties and I wanted to ask him about it," I said.

Gregg was on the phone minutes later. "I'll resign," he said. "I'm not about to be fired."

A telephone call came from the Browns the next morning. All they would say was that a press conference would be held at noon.

One sportscaster close to Gregg went on the air saying that the coach would be retained. I went out to the Baldwin-Wallace College headquarters feeling a bit of trepidation.

Modell and Peter Hadhazy, his top aide, finally came down after a rather lengthy meeting in Gregg's office. I never had it confirmed, but heard that Gregg almost persuaded the owner to keep him on.

Modell announced that Gregg had resigned and added: "We have one man [to coach] in mind. He doesn't know we're interested and this doesn't preclude seeing others."

Asked the reason for requesting Gregg's resignation, Modell said: "I don't want to have any post-mortem; no autopsy. Forrest Gregg leaves here with our best wishes."

Hadhazy, a friend and tennis partner of mine at NFL meetings, wasn't happy about the story coming out prematurely in the *Plain Dealer*.

"I'll tell you this," he said. "You'll never guess who the new coach will be. I guarantee that."

Gregg, appearing calm and rested, held a press conference the next day with wife Barbara at his side and son Forrest Jr. in the audience. He talked at length of his years in Cleveland and said the last game "was taken out of my hands."

Then he added, "I leave here unashamed of the job I did."

Barbara shed a few tears but was gracious, too.

I went back to the office that day and started to ponder the list of possibilities for the coaching post. I knew of Modell's high regard for Don Shula, but the former Brown was under contract with the Miami Dolphins. I thought of Paul Wiggin, Monte Clark and Notre Dame's Ara Parseghian, retired from college football and also a former Brown.

Then the phone rang. The caller remained anonymous, but said he wanted to give me the name of the next Browns coach.

"I'm just about sure it will be Sam Rutigliano," he said. "Check it out."

I did just that with sources in New Orleans, where Rutigliano was on Hank Stram's staff with the Saints. He also had coached at New England and I checked with people there.

I discovered that he was a very close friend of Hadhazy's. Hadhazy came to the Browns from the Patriots.

"Sam is class with a capital K," said Bob Roessler, sports editor of the New Orleans Times-Picayune. "He's extremely talented. He's not a coach. He's a professor."

My Plain Talk column in the *Plain Dealer* the next day (Dec. 15) was headed "Is it Sam?"

And it was Rutigliano who quickly sold himself to Modell and was given a three-year contract two days after Christmas.

Gregg now is athletic director at Southern Methodist, his alma mater, after coaching in Canada, Cincinnati and Green Bay, and at SMU. Modzelewski, who coached the Browns in a 20-19 loss in Seattle, had other coaching jobs with the New York Giants, Cincinnati, Green Bay and Detroit but now is retired in North Carolina. And Rutigliano, who still has a home in Cleveland, is coach of Liberty University in Lynchburg, Va.

A few months later the *Plain Dealer* shook up the sports department. I went off the Browns beat, but would continue to write my Plain Talk and Off The Cuff columns.

When I learned of the changes, I mentioned to Tom Vail, then editor and publisher, about my recent roll on the Browns beat.

"That's the way to go out," he said. "On top."

I guess he was right.

# Kono, Murphy Brought Good Times to Browns

OVER THE YEARS I noticed that the Browns played best when the players were loose and cool. They often had Leo and Morrie to thank for that.

That is, Leo Murphy, former longtime trainer, and Morrie Kono, ex-equipment manager and one of the team's original members. Both are retired.

In addition to being first-rate at their jobs, they brought fun to the locker room and the practice field. Football is big business, but you have to be a kid at heart to play it or be around it.

Murphy, who paid a visit to the Berea complex last week, still is recuperating after having a hip replacement. He is walking with a cane but is looking forward to golfing next summer.

The players didn't mind an occasional blast of cigar smoke in their faces as Murphy taped ankles or took a pulse. They forgot pain with his stories about Notre Dame, his alma mater, his first days as trainer in the All-America Conference and the early Browns.

Murphy worked hard at his job but also loved a good time. He used to enjoy lifting a Canadian Club and water or two when his tasks were done. If there was a piano present, he was glad to play a tune or two—maybe even the Irish fight song.

Murphy was 26 when he joined the team as trainer. He learned his trade as a student trainer at Notre Dame.

He was hired by Paul Brown after an interview in Philadelphia, where NFL owners were meeting in 1950.

"Betty [his late wife] and I were having breakfast in the hotel when Paul came by," Murphy said. "I was so flustered at meeting him that I never asked him to sit down.

"He said he was looking for a trainer. Wally Bock, who had been the Browns' trainer, was moving to the Indians."

Brown asked Murphy not to take a job until he talked to him again. A few weeks later he joined the Browns.

Murphy still recalls with fondness some of the players who were around in the early days. There was the late Buddy Young with the old Yankees and Otto Graham, Lou Groza, Marion Motley, Dante Lavelli and the rest of the early Browns.

"Buddy would never complain about any bruise, no matter how severe," Murphy said. "And the only protection he wore was a light rugby pad on his chest. Never any shoulder, hip or thigh pads. He wouldn't have worn a helmet except for the rules. A lot of the early Browns were the same way."

Murphy said his best memories come from the time when the Browns trained at Hiram College.

"It was like going home when we went there each summer," he said. "Dr. [Elmer] Jagow, the president, and Bill Hollinger of the athletic department were great people.

"Dr. Jagow loved to stop at practice a couple of times a week and sometimes he'd be wearing a Browns T-shirt. Bill would do anything to help the team—line the field, roll it, anything."

Kono was interviewed for the job in the team headquarters in the old Leader Building in downtown Cleveland in 1946. He had been in the army in World War II for five years and had spent a year in the Merchant Marine.

"How soon can you be at Bowling Green?" Brown asked him.

"When does the next bus leave?" asked Kono, who never learned to drive. True to his word, he was at that first Browns' training camp in a few hours and sent home for his clothes.

"Later, I learned that I would make $50 a week," he said. "I was the happiest guy in the world."

A stocky man who grew up in the Jewish Orphans Home on Woodland Ave., he would kid the players with a straight face.

A player would ask for a shoestring. "Which one, left or right?" Kono would demand.

He remembers one of the old-time players who was asked his shoe size. "Medium," was the reply.

In the early days, Kono would hold the blocking dummy for practice. "Often I'd have [defensive captain] Don Colo's teeth in my pocket."

Kono said players changed some over the years. "In the old days, all they wanted to do was play football and have fun," he said.

Kono was an original Brown, but not the first equipment manager. The first was Tommy Flynn, who was very, very short.

"When he was unloading our first shipment of shoulder pads, he kept falling in the box," Kono said. "Bock would have to pull him out. So they made him the mascot and I was hired."

Murphy and Kono became close friends over the years and roomed together at training camp and on the road. They also would be on the speaking circuit, telling humorous stories about the Browns at football functions.

It was good to know the pair and to have them as close friends. They'll always have a place in the lore of the team, along with Paul Brown, Art Modell and so many others.

# Ippolito Devotes His Career to Browns

DR. VIC IPPOLITO HAS seen many a football game, but always from the field or the sideline.

"I just don't enjoy them unless I'm really involved," he said. "I've done it for such a long time."

Ippolito is the only person who has been a member of the Browns since 1946, when Paul Brown organized his team at Bowling Green State University.

Ippolito was a consulting physician on a medical staff that is headed by Dr. John Bergfeld of the Cleveland Clinic.

"When I was hired, I was asked by Paul how much I should make," Ippolito said with a grin. "I said about $250, but meant for each game. At the end of the season, I got a check for $250 for all the games and was too embarrassed to tell them what I had really meant.

"I didn't get a raise until Art Modell gave me one a few years after he took over the club."

Ippolito got the job because of contacts. He was a fine football player at Cleveland Heights High School, which played Massillon. Katy Brown, wife of Paul, had a brother who played on some of those Massillon teams. Ippolito also knew Arthur (Mickey) McBride, who owned the club.

"I always liked football and said yes when they asked me," Ippolito said. "It seemed like a fun thing to do. I didn't think it would last this long."

Ippolito knows all the players well. He likes them as a group, guys such as Otto Graham, Marion Motley, Bill Willis, Lou Groza, Dante Lavelli, Mac Speedie, Mike McCormack and all the others right down through today's players.

"All the guys played their hearts out, and they still do," he said. "Football isn't the type of game in which you can slack off. If you don't go all out all the time, you get cut."

Ippolito said he vividly remembered Graham getting a fist smashed into his face in a 1953 game by Art Michalik of the San Francisco 49ers.

"It was a vicious cut and needed 15 sutures to close the gash inside his mouth," Ippolito said. "It happened just before the half. I did the work without using any pain killler but didn't expect him to go back.

"I was cleaning up some things in the dressing room and didn't get right back on the field after the half. When I did get out I looked at the lineup and there is Graham calling the signals."

The Browns won the game, 23-21.

"There were other times I had to do things in a hurry, but those guys sure could take a lot of pain," said Ippolito.

Ippolito got to know well the players who remained in Cleveland in the off-season. He still sees Bob Gain and his wife socially, as well as Groza, Lavelli and some of the other old-timers. They would come to him for treatment, and there were no bills.

Ippolito said his work with the team never has been questioned.

"From Paul Brown right down the line of coaches, I would say if a player could or couldn't play," he said. "There never was any second-guessing."

Ippolito said that drugs might have been used at times, but never with the OK of the doctors. "If the Browns took anything not prescribed by us, it was on their own," he said. "We didn't know about it."

Ippolito played football during his first year of medical school on the Western Reserve Red Cats. He was an all-Ohio choice at tailback and good enough to be sought by the Buffalo Bills.

"I had my medical degree then and decided football wasn't worth all the time it would take," he said.

At Cleveland Heights, he was a football, baseball and basketball letter-winner and ran against the famed Jesse Owens in track. While at Reserve, he played baseball in the city's Class A sandlot league.

He graduated from medical school in 1936 and joined the Browns 10 years later.

His first wife, Myrtle Allan, died in December 1955. She took part in the Ziegfeld Follies and the Carroll Vanities and won the title of Miss Cleveland in a beauty contest. Ippolito married his present wife, the former June Zidanic, about eight years after Myrtle died.

The Ippolitos have six children: Jean, Victor, Allan, Candice, Lee and Lois.

Besides the Browns, he worked for the Indians for nine years and for the Cobras soccer team for one year. He has received numerous medical and sports honors.

"If I had my life to live over, I wouldn't change a thing, as far as athletics are concerned," Ippolito said. "Athletics are good for boys and girls, and it's great that so many are taking an active part. This is the best thing in our fight against juvenile delinquency."

*(November 17, 1993)*

# Green Filled a Need
# and Lasted

PAUL BROWN WAS SEARCHING for a back to run with Jim Brown in the fall of 1962. That was the year that he traded Bobby Mitchell for the rights to Ernie Davis.

The Davis story is a sad one. Ernie was diagnosed as having leukemia at the College All-Star game and never played for the Browns. So the team needed a halfback.

Brown recalled a few seasons earlier when the Browns were overloaded with players. He had sent Willie Davis, Henry Jordan and some others to Green Bay.

Brown and Vince Lombardi had been friends for a long time. So he called the coach of the Packers and asked him what he had in the way of available backs.

"I have a fellow named Ernie Green," Lombardi said. "He looks like a pretty good all-round back, but I don't know if he'll make this team. You can take a look if you want to."

Brown decided to do just that. "We'd like to find a second halfback or fullback who can run back kickoffs and punts," he said.

So Green, 6-2 and 205 pounds, checked in the next day at the Hiram College training camp. There were only a couple of days before the Browns' game against the Pittsburgh Steelers in the first doubleheader.

Green got himself ready to return kicks and looked something like Eric Metcalf. He rolled for 167 yards.

"That big crowd [77,683] didn't throw a chill to him," said the coach. "He just grabbed the ball and took off."

Green said he was pretty excited before the game but not nervous.

"I didn't worry about fumbling," he said the next week. "If I can get a hand on the football I feel that I can catch it. Don't give me all the credit for those runs. Did you notice the wall of blockers around me? All I did was use the interference."

That run opened Brown's eyes and the former University of Louisville player got some time at running back the next week.

A 14th-round pick by the Packers, Green knew that with Jim Taylor, Paul Hornung, Tom Moore and others dotting the roster he probably wouldn't stick. So he said one day this week that he was happy to come to Cleveland.

"The news that I had been traded to the Browns didn't surprise or disappoint me," he said. "I was happy to go some place where a running back was needed even if they had a Jim Brown."

Green was shaken up early the next game and didn't get tested much that season. He made the club that first year mostly as a kick returner. It was the next season that he settled in as Jim's running mate and played well through 1968 when he retired.

"I did a lot of blocking over those years with Jim Brown and Leroy Kelly there," he remembered. "A back would like to carry the ball but we had a good football team and that satisfied me."

Green wound up with 3,204 yards rushing and ranks sixth in club history behind Brown, Leroy Kelly, Mike Pruitt, Greg Pruitt and Kevin Mack. He was much more than just a blocker.

"Not bad for a blocker, I guess," he said recently, evaluating his performance with a smile.

Green, who lives in Dayton, kept busy in the off-season while playing football. He entered the executive training program of the former Halle Brothers Co.

"That was a good experience and training," he said. "My wife [Wylene] also taught school in Cleveland."

The Greens have three children, Zachary, Derek and Ernie, Jr. They all have doctorate or master's degrees.

"I had several jobs before I took this one in Dayton," Green said. "I worked for Case-Western Reserve for four years helping run the school's student activities.

"Then I went with McCormack [Mark H. McCormack and Co.] and worked on team sports."

Finally, he went to Dayton, where he is president of E.G.I. (Ernie Green Industries).

"We work with all the automotive plants making various parts for the cars," he said. "Everything has been going pretty well."

When he comes to Akron's Firestone Club to play in the annual Browns golf tournament former teammates joke with him about being a millionaire. But he laughs that off.

"I'm just keeping my head above water," he said. "I make enough to pay the school bills. They all cost a lot now as you must know. That's finally over."

And did he learn something from football besides blocking, running for touchdowns and knocking someone down?

"It's a great game but you really can learn a lot from it," he said. "You learn about relationships with other people and working with teammates.

"If you can get by without being hurt seriously it's a great learning experience."

# Hickerson, Kelly Await Ultimate Christmas Gift

December 15, 1993

CHRISTMAS JOY COMES FROM the giving and anticipation. It's the same with the announcement soon to come from the Pro Football Hall of Fame in Canton. Fifteen players will be on the list and as many as eight could be taken into the Hall the day before the Super Bowl, Jan. 29, in Atlanta.

This is the 33rd year for the Hall and I've been a member of the selection committee all that time. I also am on the Seniors Committee that picked one man from a list of 20 at a meeting in Canton in June.

The Seniors Committee, originally called the Old-Timers Committee, was created in 1971 to scrutinize those whose careers occurred shortly before 1943. Now the group considers those candidates who completed at least 60 percent of their careers 25 years before the induction date. That means to be eligible, a Seniors nominee this year would complete 60 percent by 1969.

All balloting is secret and the finalists won't be known until it is announced a couple of weeks before the Super Bowl.

Over the years the Browns have had two players as standouts in this Christmas lottery. They are guard Gene Hickerson, who has been a seniors nominee for several years, and running back Leroy Kelly, who just became a senior.

Both did well during the years on the regular group. They made the final 15 a number of times but never had the best Christmas present of all—selection to the Hall.

People keep asking me when these two are going to make it. I keep telling them that they always have had my vote but came up a little short of the others.

Sportscaster Doug Dieken, a mighty fine offensive tackle and a teammate of Hickerson, kids me about not pushing hard enough. "He introduces me as the guy who can get Hickerson into the Hall if he really wants to." He knows that's just a joke.

Jim Brown's great presence on the Browns has had something to do with the chances of both. Hickerson gained prominence as a blocker for Brown and frequently was pictured leading the famed Brown sweep. Hickerson was very good but playing with Brown gave him added blocking incentive and made him even better.

With Kelly it's just the opposite. His career was shortened by the fact that the famed Brown was around for his first two seasons, 1964 and 1965.

The first of those seasons was the last championship for the Browns. In 1965 the Cleveland team lost to Green Bay.

When Brown decided to continue his film career in the summer of 1966 there was no panic among Blanton Collier and his coaching staff. They all were absolutely confident that Kelly could do the job. He responded by making the Pro Bowl teams in each of those first four seasons, 1966 through 1969.

In contrast, in 1964 and 1965 he played primarily on the special teams in those conference title games.

Hickerson is a familiar figure around the Cleveland area. He started his own business during his playing days and still is a very successful manufacturer's representative.

Present at most of the Browns' activities, he lives in Avon, where he has a tomato garden.

He was inducted into the Cleveland Sports Stars Hall of Fame in June.

Kelly coached and played in the United States Football League after finishing with the Browns. He now is a working owner of a fast food franchise in Philadelphia.

Hickerson has never said anything to me about not going into the Hall of Fame although I'm sure he knows that I do the Cleveland voting. Kelly hasn't but has told friends he believes his being overlooked is a mistake.

One of them could be very happy this holiday season by being elected but only one. The Seniors Committee nominates only one person and that person must then be accepted by the entire committee during Super Bowl weekend.

Results of voting on the final 15 will be announced Jan. 30 in Atlanta. The group of senior nominees was one of the strongest yet and included such candidates as quarterback John Brodie of San Francisco and former East Tech standout Bob Brown, who played tackle for 10 seasons for the Philadelphia Eagles, the Los Angles Rams and the Oakland Raiders.

Selection will be a little late for a Christmas gift but nevertheless very deeply appreciated by the lucky person.

*Editor's note: Leroy Kelly was inducted into the Pro Football Hall of Fame in 1994. Gene Hickerson was inducted in 2007.*

# RIVALS

# Browns-Bengals Rivalry
# Arranged in a Hospital

BROWNS PRESIDENT ART MODELL was lying in a bed in Doctors Hospital in Manhattan suffering from a bleeding ulcer. Wellington Mara, president of the New York Giants, along with Pittsburgh's Art and Dan Rooney, were standing at his side.

That was the setting for the agreement between the Cleveland Browns and Cincinnati Bengals to meet twice each year.

The two teams met three times in 1970 to get things started. Before that, it was a long haul to realign the National Football League and make this rivalry possible.

The owners caucused in March, 1969 in Palm Springs, Calif., and agreed on a merger of the NFL and the American Football League. The tough question was which teams should be in which conferences.

There were so many old rivalries to consider. Some sentiment arose for 16 teams in the NFL and 10 in the AFC.

The meeting adjourned without a solution. The owners came together two months later at the St. Regis Hotel in Manhattan, but ran into another stalemate.

Commissioner Pete Rozelle called for a locked-door bargaining session. It lasted about 40 hours with no signs of a compromise.

Modell, who collapsed in his hotel room because of the ulcer, was taken to the hospital by Tex Schramm of the Dallas Cowboys and Rozelle, who volunteered to drive Modell instead of transporting him by ambulance. While being treated, he kept in touch with negotiations by phone.

Mara and Art Rooney, owner of the Steelers, along with his son Dan, who was general manager, brought news of a suggested compromise to Modell in the hospital.

"I can still see the three of them standing next to the bed," Modell said recently. "I said the Browns would move only if Wellington agreed to it and if the Steelers came along.

"We had such a great rivalry with the Giants at the time and I knew it was important to Wellington. Our games with the Steelers usually met their payroll.

"Dan Rooney didn't want to move to the AFL, but his dad took a puff on that big cigar he always had in his mouth and said, 'I'm going with Art of a suggested compromise to Modell in the hospital.

The move was made more attractive to the Browns, Steelers and the Baltimore Colts, who also switched, when the pot was sweetened with $3 million for each of the transferring teams.

"I have regretted that we didn't include Buffalo instead of Houston," Modell said. "But that was before they had their new stadium."

Fans of the Browns and Bengals buzzed in anticipation when the schedule came out for 1970. Not only would there be two regular-season games, but also an exhibition at Riverfront Stadium.

The exhibition became much more than that. It was Paul Brown, who had been fired by Modell, against the owner and Blanton Collier. Before replacing Brown as coach in 1963, Collier was a longtime assistant to the Hall of Fame coach.

The Bengals fell behind, 14-0, in the first quarter of that exhibition, played before a capacity crowd, but rallied behind the leadership of a young quarterback named Sam Wyche to take a 17-14 lead. The Browns tied the game in the third quarter, but the Bengals came back with two touchdowns to win, 31-24.

There was much ado in the media about the omission of the handshake between Brown and Collier after that game and after the teams split the two regular-season meetings.

Brown wrote in his book *PB: The Paul Brown Story* that he talked to Collier before the game in Cleveland and said, "If there are any congratulations to be tendered, I'm offering them now."

Collier's daughter, Kay Collier Sloan, in her book *Football's*

*Gentle Giant, The Blanton Collier Story,* quoted her father as saying, "I'll start toward the center of the field. If he wants to shake, I'll shake. If he doesn't, I'll understand."

Now that both men are gone, what happened then seems unimportant. And Modell is older, and probably wiser, as he looks back on those days when the games were billed as Modell and Collier against Brown.

The sad part was that the long friendship of Brown and Collier never was renewed before Collier's death in 1983. Brown died in 1991, but the rivalry of the Browns and Bengals continues to thrive.

# Browns Lost to Steelers in 1954 and 1964 Title Seasons

THE BROWNS HAVE HAD excellent success against the Pittsburgh Steelers, one of their oldest rivals, since the competition first started in 1950.

But two defeats stand out in my memory.

With Jim Finks leading the offense at quarterback, the Steelers upset Otto Graham and the Browns, 55-27, at Forbes Field in 1954. In 1964, the Steelers came to the Stadium as decided underdogs again and won, 23-7, with Hall of Famer John Henry Johnson rolling for 200 yards and three touchdowns.

Maybe I recall the 1954 setback so well because it was my first year as the "beat" writer with the team. Paul Brown's club had dropped a 17-16 decision to the Detroit Lions in the NFL title game the previous season and they were 1-1 going into the game in Pittsburgh.

The team was housed at the old Schenley Hotel, probably the most elegant hostelry in Pittsburgh at the time.

Forbes Field was about a quarter mile from the hotel. En route to the old baseball park, a group of writers stopped for dinner at the Schenley Park restaurant, where many of the Steelers' fans gathered before the game.

The Browns were a big draw and an overflow crowd of 33,262 crowded into the stands. Even though the Steelers were 2-1, there were few Pittsburgh fans in the restaurant who gave their team much of a chance.

Last week in a telephone conversation, Finks didn't recall any unusual offensive or defensive plans by Pittsburgh coach Walt Kiesling and his staff.

"Do I remember the game?" asked Finks. "You don't forget

a victory like that one. I think Otto had only one ball hit the ground. They were completions or interceptions and he had four intercepted."

Finks remembered what Brown reportedly said after the defeat: "Even a rotten tomato explodes once in a while. It goes against everyone."

As the game neared completion, Finks knelt in the huddle to call a play and said, "Guys, I'm in ecstasy." One of his less erudite offensive lineman responded, "On what count?"

I took a late train back to Cleveland and it was jammed with disappointed Browns' fans. Some, easing the pain with alcohol, decided that Graham was over the hill and that George Ratterman, the backup quarterback, should be the starter.

The 1964 game, played on a chilly Saturday night in October, was the third against the Steelers for Blanton Collier, who was in his second year as head coach. The Browns had won three and tied the St. Louis Cardinals while the Steelers were 2-2 under Buddy Parker.

Parker complained before the game about the injury deluge that had hit his linebackers. He didn't think he would have three healthy ones to play. And he heaped praise on the Browns as one of the powers of the league.

I finished a Plain Talk column with this paragraph: "And we might add that he [Parker] has been known to blow up the opposition in the past, then take special delight in bursting the balloon."

Nevertheless, most of the 80,530 on the lakefront that night were anticipating a Cleveland romp.

Parker used an unorthodox defense of six men on the line most of the time. And Johnson, 35, romped for touchdowns of 33, 48 and 5 yards. He recently called it "my greatest game."

To shore up the defense and compensate for ailing linebackers, Parker, an astute coach, used three tackles most of the time. He had Clendon Thomas, a defensive back, operating at linebacker. John Baker, a defensive end, dropped off the line and played linebacker part of the time. The setup confused the Browns' offensive line and its normal blocking schemes.

Johnson lives in the University Circle area with wife, Leona, and has been suffering from Alzheimer's disease for two years. His long term memory still is good and he hasn't forgotten those 200 yards and a game that helped him make the Pro Football Hall of Fame.

"We didn't adjust to their unusual defense very well," said Collier after the loss. "We played very poorly in all departments."

The team had planned to hold a victory party at the old Cleveland Hotel after the game. It turned out to be more of a wake.

The Browns, however, went on to greater things in 1954 and 1964.

They went on to win NFL crowns both seasons, defeating Detroit in 1954 and Baltimore in 1964.

# Steelers' Rooney Unforgettable

THERE HAVE BEEN MANY pleasant perks from covering sports over the years: The best seats in the house, sometimes; travel expenses paid by the *Plain Dealer*; seeing so much drama unfold on the field and in the locker room.

All of this has been great. But perhaps best of all has been meeting so many grand people involved in sports, from ball boys to presidents.

There have been far too many to even try to mention all of them, but I'm often reminded of the man many in Pittsburgh called Chief.

Just as Paul Brown's death removed something from the rivalry between the Browns and Cincinnati Bengals, so did the death of Arthur J. Rooney take away from the Steelers-Browns rivalry. It's not the same without the kindly Pittsburgh owner either visiting the press box on the lakefront or having his bacon and eggs in the media room before kickoff at Three Rivers Stadium.

I recall my first meeting with him in the early 1950s. It was in a press box, of course, as that was one of his favorite habitats.

The Steelers then called Forbes Field, where the Pittsburgh Pirates also played, home. The football writers sat in a cubicle hanging out over the field. You had to duck your head under steel beams to move about the area.

Rooney had a seat in the corner where he watched the games with a Pittsburgh writer named Bob Drum. Yes, that's the same Bob Drum who went on to cover televised golf tournaments.

Seeing a newcomer on the Browns beat, the Chief immediately came over with a welcome. He stayed and chatted for a while and it was like I'd known him all my life.

Rooney knew just about all the writers who came in to cover the Steelers on a first-name basis. It seemed, however, if each of us was someone special to him.

He liked to talk sports, but he had a genuine personal interest. He would inquire about my family and other Cleveland friends in the business.

Over the years he always would ask about two of his Cleveland favorites—*Plain Dealer* sports columnists Jim Doyle and Gordon Cobbledick.

There was a period when I was ill and off the pro football beat for several weeks. Somehow he found out and sent me a handwritten note and, knowing that I was also Catholic, said that he had asked some of his friends in a religious order to pray for me. He did the same when my first wife died in 1971.

Rooney loved football, but he probably was even more enamored with horse racing. He never forgot that he made the money, or so the story goes, to buy the Steelers in one big betting afternoon at the track.

The Kentucky Derby was his favorite race and he was a regular at Churchill Downs on that first Saturday in May. He had a set routine: Mass at the Cathedral of the Assumption on Saturday morning, the Downs on Saturday afternoon, Hasenour's German restaurant Saturday night. Before leaving for Pittsburgh on Sunday, win or lose, he would stop at St. Louis Bertrand Church.

Rooney had a friend in Louisville who took time off each year to drive him about just because he enjoyed the Chief's company.

Occasionally he would fly in for the day, as he did in 1968 when Forward Pass was one of the favorites. Browns owner Art Modell picked Rooney and some friends up in Pittsburgh. Nobody had the winner, which later turned out to be Forward Pass on a disqualification, but that didn't stop the return trip from being perfect.

They waited for *Cleveland Press* Sports Editor Bob August and myself and brought us home on a starlit night. It was one of my best airplane rides.

Steelers' Hall of Fame linebacker Jack Lambert was Rooney's type of football player, although the Chief seemed to truly love anyone who wore the black and gold. When Lambert's daughter Lauren was born, she received a note from Rooney. Lambert hasn't forgotten the contents or that it was hand written.

"He wrote about what a great man her father is and what a nice woman her mother is. And he enclosed a check 'Something for your dad to buy you something with,'" Lambert said.

"The check was really significant, but the letter is something she always will be able to have. He really was unbelievable when you think about it."

Steelers running back coach Dick Hoak suffered a severe head injury late in his playing career. He said Rooney visited him at Divine Providence Hospital every morning and every night he was there.

But Rooney also liked the little people—the equipment men, the ball boys, the groundskeepers, the cleaning ladies and all the others. I used to lunch with him occasionally on visits to Pittsburgh. We would walk from his office, the door of which always was open, through the various corridors to the Allegheny Club in Three Rivers.

Along the way he always would greet the people we met by name.

"There weren't any big people and little people to Mr. Rooney," said Mary Regan, his longtime secretary. "There were just people and he wanted to help everyone. I never saw him say no to anyone in need."

Rooney had more downs than ups with his football team in the early years. So there wasn't a jealous owner in the NFL when he picked up four Super Bowl trophies. They all knew he earned them.

Now there is a larger than life statue of him in front of Three Rivers Stadium so people won't forget. But his legacy is such that he won't need a statue to be remembered.

# Bum Phillips
# Was a Class Act

IF YOU ARE IN the sportswriting business very long, you see many football coaches come and go. Usually, it wasn't a complete surprise, even in the case of the late Paul Brown, for those close to a team.

I have to admit, however, that it was more than a mild shock on New Year's Eve 1980, when O.A. (Bum) Phillips was "relieved of his duties" as the statement from the Houston Oilers read. His team had gone 11-5 that season before losing to the Oakland Raiders in a wild-card playoff game.

That was the same Raiders team that beat the Browns, 14-12, the next week at the Stadium in a game remembered for quarterback Brian Sipe's errant pass late in the game. Oakland became the only wild-card team to win a Super Bowl when it beat the Philadelphia Eagles, 27-10, in New Orleans.

By then, Phillips was looking for another job, which he found the next year in New Orleans. But he never had the success with the Saints that he enjoyed in Houston.

Phillips' record with the Oilers from 1975 through 1980 was 55-35, a .601 winning percentage. Compared with the Browns' coaches through the years, he would be second only to Brown (.759) and the late Blanton Collier (.675).

But more than his victories and defeats, the crew-cut Phillips, who wore a white cowboy hat, boots, blue jeans, string tie, wire-rim glasses and usually had a chaw of tobacco in his jaw, was an ideal representative for a Texas team. He seemed as much a part of Oilers football as the derrick symbol on the helmets.

He never looked like a bum, but his nickname seemed to suit him. It came from his youth, when his little sister tried to say "brother" and it came out "Bumble." That later was shortened to Bum. And with the baptismal names of Oail Andrew, who wouldn't prefer to be called Bum?

Phillips was more than just a competent football coach. He was a super person who treated everybody—even the media—kindly.

Of the media, he said one day last week: "I knew they had a job to do and wouldn't always agree with me. But that didn't mean we couldn't be friends."

Timing is everything in coaching, as in life. Phillips made the mistake of having his best clubs during the era when the division rival Pittsburgh Steelers were winning Super Bowls. "The road to the Super Bowl goes through Pittsburgh," Phillips used to say. "We gotta kick that door down."

He wasn't able to break through, though, and in 1978 and 1979, he lost to the Steelers in the AFC title game. The next season, he was fired.

Fullback Earl Campbell, still one of Phillips' closest friends, followed him to New Orleans, but success was not part of the contingent. Phillips resigned as Saints coach after the 12th game of the 1985 season, forgoing the final three years and $1.3 million of his contract.

Most coaches wait to be fired so they can continue to collect in retirement. But Phillips isn't that kind of person.

"I got tired of watching practice, and you practice a lot," he said. "Football ceases to be fun, and when it ceases to be fun, you ought to get out of it. I loved the games, but unfortunately, there's more to it than just the game."

Phillips got almost completely away from football after leaving the Saints. He leased several ranches and raised cattle.

"I don't miss it," he said of coaching. "If there is one thing that football teaches you it's that when the game is finished, it's over. There's no looking back."

Of the cattle business, he said: "It's like any other small business you get into. You fight to keep your head above water the first year. You can make it if you lease the land, do the work your-self and the neighbors help each other out."

Phillips was so busy riding the range after his retirement from football that he got almost completely away from the game. His wife, Helen, used to have to tell him how the Philadelphia Eagles, which had son Wade as defensive coordinator, did the previous day.

Upset when fired by the Oilers, Phillips didn't follow the team closely, although he moved back to Houston. But that has changed now with Jack Pardee, whom he coached as an assistant coach to Paul (Bear) Bryant at Texas A&M, as coach of the Oilers.

Phillips works weekends as a radio analyst for the Houston games. "I feel at home there with Jack and Mike McClure [execu-tive vice president-administration], and I'm working with two real nice young people [Tom Franklin and John O'Reilly]," Phil-lips said. "I don't have to say much."

Phillips said he always looking forward to seeing Art Modell.

"I always liked him as an owner and a person," Phillips said. "When we played in Cleveland, he almost always would come into our dressing room to say hello. He always made it if we won.

"He's also a very funny man. I love his sense of humor. As an owner, I rate him right up there with Art Rooney [late owner of the Steelers] and Wellington Mara [an owner of the New York Giants]. All three are mighty fine people."

As a coach, Phillips rates with the real fine people in the busi-ness.

# Glanville's Humor Was Oilers' Trademark

When Jerry Glanville came to Cleveland, there were tickets left for Elvis Presley, James Dean or the Phantom of the Opera.

There were one-man shopping sprees at Higbee's on Public Square.

There were nails pounded into the visitors' dressing room at the Stadium for clothes hooks.

There were jokes about Cleveland weather, a sensitive subject for many living on the shores of Lake Erie.

And the whole affair was so much fun.

The Oilers often hit the Cleveland area around the Christmas season.

"Christmas wouldn't be Christmas without me doing my shopping in Cleveland," Glanville told me once. "They seem to arrange the schedule so I can do my shopping at Higbee's. Somebody at the store takes me up to where all those expensive things are, but then I sneak down to the basement and try to find something on sale."

As to the Cleveland weather, Glanville once said, "I never thought I would root for Cleveland except to root for them to have two sunny days in a year."

And speaking further about Cleveland's lack of sunshine, he once said before a game: "The weather in Cleveland won't be that much of a factor. It's not like we're going there to live. Like I tell the people in Houston, nobody goes to Cleveland to retire."

Glanville was pretty much unique in the bland world of NFL coaches where many are afraid even to reveal a middle initial. He is the kind of a guy you either love or hate. Sort of another Howard Cosell.

I've always enjoyed his straight-faced humor and felt that he was also a good coach.

Between jobs in 1989, Glanville forgot his fun feuding with Modell and applied for the Browns' vacancy. Modell told Glanville he was flattered with his interest in the Browns, but that was the end of it.

Bud Carson, one of Glanville's closest friends from their days together at Georgia Tech, got the job only to be fired after a year and a half. Glanville proved a prophet while Carson was sitting out half of the 1990 season.

"If he wants another coaching job he won't have any trouble finding it," Glanville said. Carson found a home as defensive coordinator for the Philadelphia Eagles.

His friends say Glanville likes his tough-guy image and his feuding with other coaches, particularly Pittsburgh's Chuck Noll and Cincinnati's Sam Wyche. He seems to think it enhances his image to wear black on the field. He even has added a cowboy hat since going to Atlanta, but that's to protect his ruddy complexion from the sun after several bouts with skin cancer.

He also took up riding a motorcycle and got into car racing in the off-season. His cars were all black, of course, as was his cycle.

There is another side to Glanville, who has said: "All I care about is winning. I don't care about one other thing in football."

He's a man who liked to help people, particularly underprivileged or ailing children. He made weekly visits to hospitals to visit children. And even during the rush of the season, he took time to help feed and clothe the homeless and to provide recreation for inner-city kids.

All in all, I truly believe he is one of the most unusual, if not *the* most unusual, person I've met in the football coaching fraternity. He was been great for the media, always looking for someone unusual, but also a very good human being, corny jokes and all.

# Noll's Love for Football Shared with Hobbies

THE MOST ENJOYABLE TIME I've spent with Pittsburgh Steelers coach Chuck Noll came in the summers when I went to the Steelers' training camp at St. Vincent College in Latrobe, Pa. He always seemed to be completely relaxed there and fully enjoyed himself.

"I guess I like this part of football more than any other," he said on numerous occasions while he was relaxing at the end of the day. "Football coaching is essentially a teaching job. Training camp really is the only place where you have time to do any real teaching.

"And you have the young players here who still are in the learning stage. Many of them are good pupils. They have the intelligence and the desire."

Noll usually met the media almost every night of camp before dinner. He would climb the hill after the afternoon practice to a small recreation room at the school.

How the practice went was only one of the items discussed. He has had many hobbies over the years and didn't mind pontificating on them.

Flying became his passion for a while and he was somewhat obsessed with it. He and Pittsburgh part owner and President Dan Rooney shared ownership of a plane for a while after both became pilots.

I remember making a visit after New York Yankees catcher Thurman Munson was killed when his plane, which he piloted, crashed in 1979. Noll talked a lot about it. Not long after he pretty much gave up flying his plane.

But there were other things that intrigued his fertile mind. Music was one of his favorite topics and he became a fan of the Pittsburgh Symphony Orchestra.

"I enjoy watching the different techniques of the conductors," he once said. "It's not easy. Just about the same as coaching. The conductor is only as good as his talent.

Flowers, gourmet food and wines have come under Noll's intense scrutiny in the off-season. He and wife Marianne have grown orchids in a small greenhouse adjacent to their home. They still live in the unpretentious dwelling in Upper St. Clair, where they settled down when he took the Pittsburgh reins in 1969 at the age of 37.

While Noll is a quiet, introspective almost shy person, Marianne is outgoing, vivacious and very friendly. She was a high school cheerleader in Portsmouth, O.

She met Noll while he was playing for the Browns and she was a medical secretary at the Cleveland Clinic. They became close friends of the Indians' Rudy Regalado and his wife and still are. Son Chris is a prep school teacher in New England.

As a guard, Paul Brown, the late coach of the Browns and founder of the Cincinnati Bengals, often compared Noll with Lin Houston, one of the original messenger guards. That, indeed, was high praise.

Watching Noll over the years as a player and coach, I see him as being the closest to the Paul Brown image as anyone who came under P.B.'s influence. When he spoke of quarterback Terry Bradshaw and others, saying that it "may be time for him to get about his life's work," it seemed like P.B. talking.

Four Super Bowl rings haven't changed the man I first became aware of when he was a high school lineman on Benedictine's *Plain Dealer* Charity Game champions in 1948.

Like Brown, it's football, family and religion and not necessarily in that order. He has no radio show, no TV show, few speaking engagements, no endorsements and is not the subject of rumors that he's about to become a TV football analyst.

"An expert is a guy who makes a statement he doesn't have to prove," Noll has said frequently.

Since forgetting his quest for a law degree and heading west to join the Los Angeles Chargers as an assistant coach in the American Football League in 1960, all he has done is coach. "These other things [endorsements, speeches, etc.] are for the players," he said. "I'm not interested."

It was in the winner of 1969, after three years as Don Shula's assistant at Baltimore, that Noll thought he was ready to become a head coach.

Art Rooney, the late Steelers owner, hadn't had much success at picking coaches. He solicited many opinions, even from sportswriters.

Rooney was told that Noll seemed to be ready, that he had paid his dues as an assistant and was bright. While with the Browns, he was called "The Pope" because he never seemed to make a mistake on the field.

Noll laughs about that nickname. "When I started out, I used to carry the plays to the quarterback while playing guard," he said. "Sometimes, I would forget part of them in the excitement, but Otto [Graham, former Browns quarterback] always knew what P.B. wanted."

Rooney narrowed his selection list to two, Noll and Nick Skorich, then offensive coordinator for the Browns. The Rooneys offered the post to Skorich, who turned it down because he was heir apparent to Blanton Collier in Cleveland.

Noll might not have been in pro football at all except for Joey (Geever) Gavin, who coached at Holy Name High School in Cleveland and became the University of Dayton's head coach. He successfully recruited Noll for the Flyers in 1949 and his strong recommendation got him his test with the Browns.

Noll has been like Brown, too, in that he remains somewhat aloof from his players. He's not a hugger or a back-slapper and some of them have resented this.

He's also not a Knute Rockne before the game or at halftime, but Bradshaw once said that Noll's short speech before the game against the Oakland Raiders for the AC title before their first Super Bowl championship in 1974 really hit the spot.

"People don't give us a chance, but we're going out there and beat those SOBs," he told his players. The Steelers won, 24-13, in Oakland, Calif.

# Lambert Stood Out
# on Dominant Steelers

THE BROWNS FINISHING THE 1992 season against the Steelers in Pittsburgh reminded me that I spent much time over the years at Three Rivers Stadium. Coach Chuck Noll's squads were dominant, with Super Bowl rings a Christmas present on four occasions and the NFL playoffs an annual expectation.

With Art and Dan Rooney as the owners and Noll at the helm, the welcome mat always was out for this visitor from Cleveland. I got to know the players well with trips to the St. Vincent College training camp in Latrobe, Pa., as part of the annual schedule.

(Mean) Joe Greene, who only lived up to that tag on the football field, told me I should rent an apartment in Pittsburgh. He always was a good interview. So was quarterback Terry Bradshaw, who usually had a chaw of tobacco in his mouth and liked to play cards while at camp.

Others who gathered in the spacious Three Rivers locker room over the years were mostly pleasant people in victory or defeat. But the player who interested me the most and that I probably enjoyed most was Jack Lambert. I have seen some great linebackers over my years, but I believe he is the best I watched.

He played with more intensity than any I have seen and always was around the ball. And he could handle pass coverage as well as stuff up the middle.

When I first met him as a rookie in 1974, he called me Mr. Heaton, but he graduated to Chuck in later years.

He had a locker at the back of the room at Three Rivers. On every visit, I'd go over and have a brief chat if it wasn't game day. And no matter the score, he would answer questions after the game.

On some visits to Cleveland, the Steelers stayed at the Marriott Hotel near the airport. He and his dad and some of his buddies would eat at the Iron Gate restaurant in Rocky River.

Lambert was delighted early with a house specialty—the turtle soup—and asked the waitress for the recipe. He was told that it was the chef's secret and never divulged.

Lambert made his way to the kitchen and en route took out the partial plate that made up for some missing front teeth. Then, using that steely stare that was as scary as his play, he demanded the turtle-soup fixings.

He was only kidding, of course. The chef knew it and just grinned, but he handed over the recipe and got an autograph on a napkin in return.

It was in June 1981 that I decided that I and the *Plain Dealer* readers should know this future Hall of Famer better. He had been in seven straight Pro Bowls at the time.

So I asked Joe Gordon, then the Steelers' publicity director, for an off-season meeting. On the first day of summer, I arrived at Three Rivers to see his shiny black Cherokee jeep parked in front.

*PD* photographer Dick Conway and I had gotten lost and were a little late for the 11 a.m. meeting. Lambert put on his game-day scowl and greeted us with, "When I say 11 o'clock, I mean 11."

Then he smiled and suggested we follow him to his suburban home. He was living in an exclusive suburb called Fox Chapel, about a half hour from Pittsburgh's Golden Triangle.

"I need rest after the season," he said, "and I find it here. Yep, I've even become a bird watcher. Even saw a purple finch the other day and was excited about it."

The tour of the house uncovered football mementos dating back to his football days at Crestwood High School in Mantua, O. He remembered how he visited Hiram to watch the Browns work while in high school and at Kent State.

Over the years, he sacked Browns quarterback Brian Sipe quite a few times. Then he met Sipe at the Pro Bowl.

"I was surprised how small he is off the field," Lambert said. "I admire his guts. He'll take a shot."

Lambert always had the spare seconds to give a kid an autograph. He said it may go back to a Hiram visit when a tired and dusty Jim Brown stopped to give him, a high school student, his signature.

Few players enjoy training camp, but Lambert's time at St. Vincent was made more pleasant by his friendship with Father Raymond, one of the oldest monks.

"I met him my rookie year and have been seeing him ever since," he said. "He must be close to 90, but he's a wise and interesting person."

It was on the visit to Fox Chapel that the bachelor Lambert said he wanted to marry and have a family if he could find someone "I can live with and who can live with me."

Now retired and in the Pro Football Hall of Fame, he found that person in wife Lisa. They have two daughters—Lauren, 7, and Elizabeth, 5. Son John Jr. was born July 8, 1991.

The Lambert home now is in Worthington, Pa., a wooded tract of 125 acres. He has become more outgoing with marriage, added years and a stint as a television commentator.

He also has taken up a new sport. He plays amateur hockey with some men in the area.

I missed him in a telephone call, but he put a message on my answering service:

"Sorry I didn't get back sooner, but this is the deer season and I'm working with the Pennsylvania Game Commission as a deputy wildlife conservation officer. It's been keeping me busy, but I know you can write about the Browns and Steelers without talking to me again. Hope you and yours have a merry Christmas."

# Beating Lions Was Never Easy for Browns

THE WORD "JINX" IS commonly used in sports. It means, of course, just what the dictionary says—"to foredoom to failure or misfortune."

Some teams seem to be in this situation when they play certain rivals, and it has been that way with the Browns against the Detroit Lions.

When the teams played for the first time in 1952, both had strong teams. They met in National Football League title games three straight times—1952-54—and again in 1957.

The first five times the teams met, Browns coach Paul Brown was matched against Detroit coach Raymond (Buddy) Parker.

Parker was a lanky Texan who made snap decisions and occasionally drank too much. He also was an excellent coach.

Detroit fans still recall the 1957 preseason welcoming luncheon put on by a booster club. After a steady string of praise from some of the boosters, Parker went to the microphone.

The coach said a few unkind things about the squad and ended up by saying he was quitting as coach. He left with a 4-1 record against Brown. George Wilson, one of his assistants, took over and beat the Browns twice in 1957, the second time, 59-14, for the title.

The Browns' 17-16 loss in the 1953 championship game in Detroit was difficult to take. The Browns were ahead going into the final minute when Detroit wide receiver Jim Doran somehow managed to get behind Browns defensive back Warren Lahr and score a touchdown.

That was the low point of a fine career for Lahr, who came to the Browns after playing quarterback at Western Reserve University.

One of the nicest people ever to wear a Browns uniform, Lahr held up well and made no excuses in the locker room. He was the same on the ride home from Detroit.

Then he and Fritz Heisler, the offensive line coach, left together for their homes in Aurora. On the ride to Aurora, Lahr broke down and cried, feeling responsible for another loss to the Lions.

The schedule called for a regular-season meeting in 1954 in Cleveland. It was meaningless for the Browns as they had already clinched a spot in the title game. Detroit won, 14-10, and became Cleveland's opponent the next Sunday at the Stadium with the crown at stake.

The Browns players began to wonder if the Lions did have them jinxed. Or did Parker have Paul Brown's number?

The night before the game, the Browns went to the old Pick Carter Hotel on Prospect Ave. as usual, but mutiny against Brown was in the air. The squad, particularly the offense, was fed up with losing. In the four games against Detroit, the most they had scored was 16 points.

Some of the key offensive players—quarterback Otto Graham, receivers Dante Lavelli, Darrell Brewster and Ray Renfro and others—decided to take things into their own hands. They met at 2:30 a.m. Sunday at the hotel.

There was talk that Brown had been too conservative in his play-calling against the tough Detroit defense. He had been using his running backs—Maurice Bassett and Curly Morrison—too much, they thought.

Brown sent the plays in with messenger guards. Graham had only minimum options to change the play at the line of scrimmage.

Graham and the offense decided to take matters into their own hands. If Brown's play-calling didn't suit them, Graham would call his own game.

"We were aware of what the consequences might be, but decided to take a chance," Lavelli said recently.

The Browns got the ball and Brown sent in a play. Surprisingly, it was for a pass. It went for a touchdown.

The next time the Browns got the ball, they hit on another pass and quickly went in for another touchdown. Brown was putting the ball in the air and calling the game the players wanted. His team went on to win, 56-10, in one of the most lopsided title games ever.

The players never told Brown of their planned rebellion. He might have known, though, as there weren't many secrets from him.

For the Browns, however, the victory was only a reprieve from their jinx against the Lions. Detroit won the next four games between the clubs, including the 1957 title game.

The Browns had an excuse in that loss. Starting quarterback Milt Plum had pulled a hamstring playing catch in the Wednesday practice and was used only briefly. The backups weren't able to do a thing against the strong Detroit defense.

# Namath Memorable in
# Victory or Defeat

WHEN ANYONE MENTIONS THE New York Jets, the name of Joe Willie Namath always pops into my mind. He isn't one of my all-time favorite athletes, but he did figure prominently in two unforgettable games I covered.

I can still see the dejected Namath, in his white shoes, head bowed, shoulders hunched, hands planted on his hips, standing at about second base in the Stadium infield on a warm September night in 1970. He never moved as Browns linebacker Billy Andrews romped 25 yards for a clinching touchdown against the Jets in the first Monday night game.

Namath somehow appeared "frail and beaten" at that moment as he was described in the book *Monday Night Mayhem*. So different than the brash signalcaller who had "guaranteed" victory over the Baltimore Colts in the third Super Bowl in Miami after the 1968 season.

There were 47 seconds remaining on that sultry night on the lakefront when the Jets took over on their 8-yard line and trailing, 24-21. It was plenty of time for a noted come-from-behind quarterback such as Namath to get his team into at least field-goal range.

"Everybody was fixing for one of his famous comebacks," Andrews, now a dairy farmer in Clinton, La., recalled recently in *Sports Illustrated*. "We just braced for it. On first down, he faded back to pass, but we got good pressure on him.

"He rolled away from the pressure. I think he was trying to throw to Emerson Boozer coming out of the backfield."

Namath probably never saw Andrews in short coverage. The ball was slightly underthrown and Andrews dove to make the catch, rolled over, and got to his feet and ran into the end zone for six points.

"I still remember everything very clearly," Andrews said. "I remember most Namath just standing there in the middle of the field with his hands on his hips and his head down. He was so stunned he never even tried to tackle me. He stood there and just stared at the ground."

That play in the national spotlight changed things for Andrews. He had gone into the game as a substitute for Dale Lindsey, now an assistant coach with Tampa Bay. Andrews soon became a regular starter and later served as a captain.

I had almost forgotten until checking some of my old scrapbooks that Homer Jones, a wide receiver and kickoff returner playing his first game for the Browns, also had a moment of glory. He took the second-half kickoff 94 yards for a touchdown.

Two longtime friends coached in that game. Weeb Ewbank, the Jets coach and Blanton Collier of the Browns were on Paul Brown's Cleveland staff in the late 1940s and early 1950s.

Nearly every Browns fan I meet tells me he or she was at that game. Many of them were as 85,703, the team's home record turnout, jammed the Stadium to see the Browns' 31-21 victory. The gate sale that night was largest in the history of the club.

Browns president Art Modell recalls that no team was eager to host that first Monday night game, not knowing if it would be received by the fans. So he, the chairman of the NFL's television committee, volunteered. He and then NFL commissioner Pete Rozelle had been discussing such a series of Monday night games for a decade. Roone Arledge, former sports chief of ABC-TV, came up with the $8.5 million for the series contract.

Personally, more memorable was my first meeting with Namath and a minor "scoop" for the *Plain Dealer*. I was in Florida to cover that third Super Bowl when Namath announced that he was not talking to sportswriters.

But Clive Rush, an old friend from Ohio, was quarterback coach for the Jets. "Come over to our hotel tomorrow and I'll have

Joe [Namath] sit down with you and Si [Si Burick, late sports editor of the *Dayton Daily News*]," Rush promised.

So Burick and I drove to the Gault Ocean Mile Hotel in Fort Lauderdale, where the Jets were housed and Rush kept his word. Namath came out to the pool in his swim trunks and we sat around for an hour or so.

The quarterback provided a readable column in which it was noted that he was "courteous to autograph seekers and seemed to have a special way with children."

During the interview, which Namath appeared to be enjoying as he sunned himself, a curvaceous blonde, clad in a pink bikini walked past. Looking with disgust at the writers she said, "Poor Joe, they just won't leave him alone."

Namath's Jets did make his "guarantee" of victory hold up in the Orange Bowl, 16-7, and he was the most valuable player. The next week, Burick and I found ourselves pictured in *Sports Illustrated* at poolside with the smiling Namath seated between us. The boss said he knew now why I always brought back such a good tan from coverage of Super Bowls in Florida.

There have been other recent memorable games with the Jets, such as the 1986 playoffs when the Browns won, 23-20, in two overtimes. But that's a memory for some other time.

# Browns-49ers Rivalry
# Dates to Pre-NFL Days

THE PITTSBURGH STEELERS BECAME the Browns' most heated rival in the early 1960s. The 1963 game, on a Saturday night at the Stadium, was a sellout, and that became the norm for Steelers visits to the lakefront.

It was different in the early days of the Cleveland franchise, when the Browns played in the All-America Conference. The most popular visitor then was the San Francisco 49ers, who never drew fewer than 70,000, except for a somewhat meaningless championship game in 1949, when only 22,550 showed up at the Stadium.

There was a reason for the lack of interest: It was a wet, nasty day, and it had been announced the day before that the AAC had merged with the National Football League. It wasn't really a merger, as only the Browns, 49ers and Baltimore Colts were taken into the NFL.

Each Browns player received $266.11 for the 21-7 title-game victory.

The 49ers have maintained an exciting team through the years, led by excellent quarterbacks. The 49ers have had such standouts as Frankie Albert, Y.A. Tittle, John Brodie, Joe Montana and now Steve Young.

Albert was a little guy by football standards, 5-9 and about 165 pounds. Also, he was left-handed.

"I think I was about 5-10 when I played at Stanford University," he said by telephone last week from California. "But they wore me down."

San Francisco owner Tony Morabito grabbed some national headlines when he signed Albert, who had led Stanford's Cinderella team to an undefeated season in 1940. Albert was given full rein by coach Buck Shaw to put his stamp of color and excitement on the 49ers.

"I guess my size was a handicap and a blessing," said Albert. "I looked for passing lanes, but when they didn't show up, I moved outside. I could scramble pretty well, particularly in the early days."

The Browns found that out.

"He was very, very quick," said Hall of Famer Bill Willis, who played both ways for a while. "He had great maneuverability and was a slick ball handler. I'd say he was something like Joe Montana has been for San Francisco."

Albert, 74, who lives in Rancho Mirage, Calif., spent three seasons as coach of the 49ers. He was asked his opinion of the quarterbacks of his era and the all-time passers.

"You know who it was when I played," he responded without hesitation. "It had to be [Otto] Graham. He was such a fine all-around athlete that he did it all for the Browns. He had a great pass touch, but some people may have forgotten how well he could run with the ball."

Albert ranked Graham right at the top, along with Montana.

The Browns went 7-2 against the 49ers in the AAC. They lost the first meeting in 1946 and the first game of the final 1949 season. The Browns lead the 49ers, 8-6, in NFL play.

"I'll never forget that 1949 regular-season game," Albert said. "We won, 56-28, before a big crowd at Kezar Stadium. We jumped out to a 28-14 lead at the half, and it went the same way after the half. I didn't have a spectacular day, but everyone on our team played well."

They weren't playing just for the money, either. Albert recalled that $17,500 was his top pay for a season.

"I remember talking salary with Tony [Morabito] one day over lunch," he said. "He wanted to pay me $15,000, and I was asking $20,000. He said that we should flip a coin and I would get the

$20,000 if I called it right. I lost, but I must have looked awfully sad, because he came up with $17,500 as a compromise."

Albert's football skills included punting. He was one of the best at the time.

*Sports Illustrated* football writer Paul Zimmerman remembers watching Albert put on a punting display at Stanford. "He would either hit or come close to towels he placed on the sideline," Zimmerman said. "He had the ball rolling right, left, forward, backwards. He could do tricks with it."

One of the first things Albert did when he was named coach in 1956 was to visit Cleveland. "I asked Paul Brown if I could come in and see how he did things," Albert said. "I wish I could have spent more time with him."

Albert resigned as coach after three average seasons and no titles. He later was a TV analyst but made his living in the real estate business.

n my Hiram College dorm room during Browns training camp back in the late 1960s. Camp ack then was almost eight grueling weeks long. It was long for the writers, too. But it was also nformal. We stayed in the same dorm building as the players. Everyone ate in the dining halls at he same time.

Interviewing Browns coach Blanton Collier (right) during a post-game press huddle. (That's me second from the right.) Blanton was a classic soft-spoken southerner, but a brilliant tactician.

Rehearsing for the annual Ribs and Roast musical spoof we used to put on for charity. We made fun of the local teams, their management, and our-selves. Everyone took themselves a lot less seriously back then. I'm in the center (with *Press* writer Bob August on the right and *Plain Dealer* sports editor Hal Lebovitz on the far right).

An old *Plain Dealer* promotional photo. You'd never see anything as good-natured as this between a team and the media today.

At Hiram College during training camp, goofing around with some photographers. (I'm in the middle.) I always had a good relationship with those guys.

Paul Brown. His players called him "The General." They feared him, but respected him, too. *(CSU)*

Otto Graham was the best quarterback the team ever had. He played in 10 championships in his 10 seasons. *(CSU)*

Mac Speedie (here with Paul Brown) was a selective receiver. He knew when he could get open and when he could beat his man. When he spoke, Graham listened. *(CSU)*

Marion Motley was an intimidating runner and a superb blocker. He took it as a personal affront if Graham came off the field with any dirt on his uniform. *(CSU)*

m Brown: the greatest running back ever
d the second most important Browns
ayer to his team, after Graham. *(CSU)*

Lou "The Toe" Groza set a record by scoring
at least one point in 107 consecutive games.
The current Browns training facility is at 76
Lou Groza Blvd. in Berea.

inning back Leroy Kelly honored me by
king if I would present him at his Hall of
me induction ceremony in 1994. It was a
ge thrill for me. *(CSU)*

Brian Sipe was the commander of the
Kardiac Kids. That was exciting football.
But it was no fun to be writing about it on
deadline. *(CSU)*

John Morrison, Paul Wiggin, myself, and Frank Ryan. We all stayed pretty good friends even after their playing days.

I'm getting my neck crushed by Mike McCormack and Bob Gain. There was a lot of good-natured kidding back in those days. Gain used to make fun of the fact that I was a daily jogger. He accused me of being a frustrated athlete.

Browns coach Nick Skorich was very good with the media. He always started a season by having the media regulars over to his home in Brecksville for a meal cooked by his wife, Theresa. We became very good friends.

With my wife of 32 years, Cece, and retired Browns trainer Leo Murphy. Leo was not only a great trainer, he could also play the piano and did a crack impression of W.C. Fields.

Art Modell around 1961. Browns fans may never forgive him for moving the team. But I do understand what an emotional person he is and how snubbed he felt when the Indians got a new stadium and he was told to go jump in the lake.

Browns coach Bill Belichick told the media they could watch practice, but not report what they saw. If the rule was violated, the practices would be closed to the media. Why couldn't he have won four Super Bowls when he was with the Browns?

I covered Don Shula when he played ball at John Carroll, when he played for the Browns, when he coached the Baltimore Colts and the Miami Dolphins. Now I watch his television commercials.

Among many thrills in my career, this one is hard to beat. I received the Pro Football Hall of Fame's Dick McCann Memorial Award in 1980.

# BIG MOMENTS

# Browns Beat Colts
# for Last Title

WHEN THE BROWNS HEAD west to play the Indianapolis Colts, it still doesn't make sense to this long-time follower of the National Football League.

They should fly east to play the Colts in Baltimore.

The Colts are Don Shula in his younger days, John Unitas at his best, Raymond Berry getting loose for a pass, fullback Alan Ameche ramming up the middle and all the others who meant so much to the franchise.

And those crabcake sandwiches in the press box at halftime in Baltimore will never be forgotten.

Indianapolis is an up-and-coming city with a revived downtown, but it should have gone after an expansion team, not the Colts. I was reminded of all this a few weeks ago when the original Colts band, still keeping alive the tradition of pro football in Baltimore, performed at a Browns game.

The Browns and Colts had some classic battles over the years. There was one in 1959 when a youthful Jim Brown ran for five touchdowns in a 38-31 Cleveland victory.

But the one never to be forgotten by Cleveland fans or this writer was Dec. 27, 1964. That was the day the Browns won their last NFL title, defeating the Colts, 27-0, at the Stadium.

The Browns stayed at a hotel the night before the game. It was the old downtown Pick-Carter Hotel on Prospect Ave.

The Colts, winners in the NFL's Western Division, came into the game with a 12-2 record. The Browns were 10-3-1, but had clinched the Eastern Division title with a 52-20 rout of the New York Giants at Yankee Stadium.

The Colts had opened on the betting line as 17-point favorites, primarily because of Unitas and the veteran team. Those odds dwindled gradually the week before the game. They were down to seven by kickoff.

As a columnist and pro football beat writer for the *Plain Dealer*, it was my duty to make a pick in the game. I was leaning toward the Colts until I made a Saturday visit to the Pick-Carter and ran into defensive ends Paul Wiggin and Bill Glass in the lobby.

"We've made some defensive changes," one of them told me. "We have some surprises for the Colts. Pick us to win and you won't go wrong."

The NFL brass had a pre-game party that evening at the Sheraton-Cleveland Hotel on Public Square. I ran into the late Tex Maule, then the NFL expert for *Sports Illustrated*.

Maule kept repeating to me how the Colts not only were going to win, but win easily. "It's a mismatch," he said.

I kept remembering how the headline on my Plain Talk column in the next day's paper was going to read: BROWNS ARE PICK AS BROWN HOLDS KEY.

My wife and I stayed at the Pick-Carter the night before the game and went to Mass with some of the players Sunday morning. Most of them seemed a little more quiet than usual.

The 18 defensive players, who were to play well, met in the hotel's Aviation Room. They were under the direction of defensive coach Howard Brinker. Defensive signal-caller and cornerback Bernie Parrish said they were going to use what was known as the "Brown Defense" unless the Colts forced them out of it.

The defense was named after Paul Brown, who had been succeeded as coach by Blanton Collier in 1963.

As Parrish explained it, this was an overshifted defense to the weak side (the side away from Baltimore tight end John Mackey). The strong-side tackle played in the gap between the guard and center. The middle linebacker moved over and lined up in the hole between the tackle and strong-side end.

Sunday morning was gray with a hint of snow in the air and a brisk breeze off the lake. The field was in good shape, however, having been covered all week with a tarpaulin. Huge blowers had been used to thaw and dry the ground.

As fate would have it, my press box seat put me next to Maule. His pre-game lecture told me how I would rue my pick.

Maule became less confident as the game progressed. Neither team scored in the first half. After the intermission, wide receiver Gary Collins made three touchdown catches to win most valuable player honors and an automobile. The passes were from quarterback Frank Ryan, who completed 11-of-18 for 206 yards.

Jim Brown ran for 114 yards on 27 carries. The first points were put on the board by 40-year-old Lou Groza with a 43-yard field goal.

The defense played beautifully in the shutout. Linebacker Galen Fiss, playing with a broken hand in a cast, had a career game. Linebacker Vince Costello and cornerback Walter Beach each intercepted Unitas. Jim Parker was putty in the hands of Browns defensive tackle Jim Kanicki.

The next day, this fearless predictor, perhaps buoyed by his success, saw the beginning of an Eastern Division domination by the Browns. They were in the NFL title game in the 1965, 1968 and 1969 seasons, but the crown and Super Bowl participation has eluded them.

# Browns Shocked Eagles, NFL in 1950 Opener

OPENING GAMES IN ALL sports are something special for players and fans. Everybody is starting even, with no losses and at least a minimum of expectations.

This is especially true in football, where fewer games are played. One loss by the Browns, who play 16 games, might be considered equivalent to 10 by the Indians, who play 162.

Probably no Browns opener created more national interest or excitement than their first game in the National Football League in 1950.

It was a great beginning to a season that ended with one of the most memorable games the club ever played—the 30-28 victory over the Los Angeles Rams at the Stadium in the NFL title game.

"I consider that season the greatest for the Browns from beginning to end," quarterback Otto Graham told me.

I never heard the late Paul Brown say it in so many words, but the way he talked about those two games and remembered the players, I have the feeling he recalled it as his most memorable opener and closer of a season.

The Browns' first NFL game was played Sept. 16, a Saturday night, under the not-too-bright lights of Philadelphia Municipal Stadium, with 71,237 fans attending.

The Eagles, coached by Earle (Greasy) Neale, were the defending NFL champions. The Browns had won four straight titles in the All America Conference.

It was similar to the first Super Bowl, when Vince Lombardi and the Green Bay Packers represented the NFL by playing the Kansas City Chiefs of the American Football League.

Graham recalled that NFL people had been saying disparaging things about the Browns and the AAC for years.

"There had been a lot of nasty remarks," he said. "We recalled those going into Philadelphia."

The Browns had been playing for four seasons in the lightly regarded All-America Conference. Coached by Paul Brown, they had won the title each year, but NFL old-timers regarded them as "cheese champs" or "upstarts" because of the caliber of the opposition.

Even the fans in Cleveland didn't know what to expect. They knew that their team had so dominated the All-America Conference that spectator interest had waned. The 1949 championship game against the San Francisco 49ers, won by Cleveland, 21-7, drew only 22,550 to the Stadium.

Some Browns followers became convinced the team would do well in the NFL, however, when the team won all five exhibition games in 1950.

The Eagles' confidence was firmly founded. They had won 11 of 12 games in 1949, losing only to the Chicago Bears, and had shut out the Los Angeles Rams, 14-0, in the title game.

The merger of the two leagues had taken place the night before the AAC championship game, but a week before the NFL playoff between the Eagles and the Rams.

Neale was so confident of his team's superiority that he didn't scout the Browns and 49ers, although he knew he would be playing one of those teams. Brown sent two of his coaches—Blanton Collier and Fritz Heisler—to watch the Rams and Eagles, who played in the rain in Los Angeles.

Brown said that he and his coaches felt more confident than ever after watching the Eagles win. They didn't see anything in the Philadelphia exhibitions to make them change their strategy.

The Eagles had built their wing-T running attack around a back destined to enter the Pro Football Hall of Fame—Steve Van Buren—but he was injured and didn't play against the Browns.

The Eagles' defense utilized a tight five-man line with two line-backers to jam the ends, and four defensive backs.

Brown had been preparing his team physically and mentally for the meeting from the end of the previous season. He wrote a letter to each player in the off-season and asked them to report to training camp at Hiram College in the best possible condition. He also had a message for them at the start of training that summer.

"We've established quite a reputation in four years," he told them. "But we've been taunted and disparaged about playing in an inferior league. We've heard that the worst team in the NFL can beat the best team in the All-America Conference.

"There is not only this coming season at stake but our four years of achievement as members of the AAC. I'm asking that you dedicate yourselves more than ever to preserve the reputations the Browns have made. It won't be easy. We're new to this league and things may get rough at times. But remember that the worst thing you can ever do to an opponent is to beat him. An opponent understands that more than anything else."

Brown told some writers of his game plan. He decided to neutralize the strong Philadelphia linebackers by putting left half-back Rex Bumgardner in motion and starting each play in a double wing formation to force single coverage. That meant Eagles defensive back Russ Craft had to take Dub Jones, a fine receiver for the Browns, man for man. Brown considered that an impossible task for Craft.

Brown also spread the Philadelphia defensive line by imperceptibly widening the split between the Cleveland guards and tackles on each successive play. With no middle linebacker in the Eagles' defense, the center of the line was the weak area.

As the Browns practiced for the game, Brown had one worry. He was afraid his team might peak too soon or be too high for the game. He recalled that the night of the game, his players quickly put on their uniforms and just stared at the dressing room walls, few saying a word. He said he never has seen a team so keyed up, so ready to play. In fact, he sent them out to the field early because he was afraid they might start hitting the lockers or concrete walls in the dressing room.

The Eagles had two good early drives but had to settle for field-goal attempts on each drive, making one. Fullback Marion Motley went in at linebacker and personally stopped one of those drives.

Soon the Cleveland passing game began to take control. Quarterback Otto Graham dissected the Eagles' defense after Philadelphia scored first on a 15-yard field goal. Graham threw to Dub Jones and Dante Lavelli for touchdowns. The passing was so effective that Brown, who called the plays, sent in only 10 runs in the first three quarters.

"P.B. [Paul Brown] didn't say much, but for four years he kept putting items on the bulletin board," Graham said. "We were so fired up for the game we would have played them (the Eagles) anywhere—for a keg of beer or a chocolate milk shake. It wouldn't have mattered.

"It was the game I remember most, the greatest game for me in my greatest year of football," Graham said.

The Browns finished the season at 10-2. The two losses were to the New York Giants, but the Browns beat the Giants, 8-3, in a playoff to get into the title game.

The Rams formerly were in Cleveland and won the NFL title in their last season here (1945). They had an excellent team led by quarterbacks Bob Waterfield and Norm Van Brocklin. Tom Fears and Glenn Davis were brilliant receivers.

The title game started ominously for the Browns when Davis took the ball into the end zone on an 82-yard pass play from Waterfield. The Browns had an unusual missed point after their second touchdown and trailed, 14-13, at the half.

They went ahead, 20-14, on a second scoring pass to Lavelli, who is a Cleveland-area businessman. But the Rams rebounded for a 28-20 lead. That lead was cut to one point when Rex Baumgardner, a running back, got loose in the end zone for what Brown once called "an unbelievable catch."

The Browns were driving again when Graham was hit on a quarterback draw and lost the ball on a fumble. The quarterback came off the field crushed because he thought he had lost the game and the title.

"I was devastated," Graham remembered. "I felt worse about that fumble than I did years later when I learned I had cancer. Paul was known for his sarcastic remarks and his steely glare but that day he patted me on the shoulder and said, 'Don't worry. We'll win this thing.'"

Graham said he had a great surge of confidence and felt it was in his voice when the Browns did hold and got the ball 68 yards from the Los Angeles goal line.

"I think the players could hear that confidence in my voice," Graham said. "I started out with a quarterback draw for 14 yards. Then I gave them some little sideline passes."

The Browns moved to the Rams' 11-yard line. They ran the ball once more and put it in the center of the field. Lou Groza dropped back from his tackle position to kick.

"The wind was blowing fiercely but I don't recall being nervous," said the Toe. "I took three deep breaths as I always did to relax. Everything was perfect, the snap from Frank [Gatski] and the hold by Tommy [James]. Tommy was a very good holder."

So the Browns won, 30-28, for the NFL title.

"It was a wonderful, wonderful season," Graham said.

# Loss in '58 Finale
# Was a Giant Pain

LONG BEFORE THE PITTSBURGH Steelers had won any Super Bowls or the Cincinnati Bengals were formed, the New York Giants were the chief rival of the Browns.

The Giants and Browns were in the Eastern Division of the National Football League. That meant home and home games each season.

It was Jim Brown against Sam Huff and the original Fearsome Foursome. It was Browns coach Paul Brown's offensive thinking against Giants defensive coordinator Tom Landry's defense.

Longtime friends Art Modell of the Browns and Wellington Mara of the Giants were adversaries at least twice a season. The two games often decided which club would play in the NFL championship game as the East's representative.

Giants Stadium in East Rutherford, N.J. wasn't even a dream in those years. The New York homes games were played in Yankee Stadium, where the crowd so menaced the Browns that on one occasion, Paul Brown took his players off the field until a semblance of order was restored.

Most memorable of all the games, and one of the all-time low points for the Cleveland club, came in the regular-season finale in December 1958. The Browns headed east needing only a tie to wrap up the title and meet the Baltimore Colts for the NFL title.

The game started well for Cleveland. Jim Brown found a big hole and raced 60 yards for a touchdown.

"We were in total shock for a moment," said Dick Modzelewski, a tackle on a Giants defensive line that included Andy Robustelli, Rosey Grier and Jim Katcavage. "I remember Tom Landry called us together and said: 'That won't happen again.' And it didn't.'"

But the Browns did get a field goal from Lou Groza to take a 10-3 halftime lead. And at the start of the second half, they moved again into chip-shot field-goal range.

But Paul Brown, in uncharacteristic fashion, called for a fake with holder Bobby Freeman trying to skirt left end for six points. Freeman slipped and went down on the slick baseball infield, but a Cleveland victory, or at least a tie, still seemed safe.

The Giants kept Jim Brown in check and tied the game, 10-10.

"He was one hell of a runner," said Modzelewski. "Our whole defense was aimed at stopping him. We had to gang tackle, powder him, to get him down. We weren't out to destroy him, but we did beat the hell out of him."

Snow began to fall in the second half as the Giants evened the score. But they needed to win to force a tie for the division title and a playoff game.

Their chances seemed to be gone when Frank Gifford appeared to fumble the ball after catching a pass. Browns linebacker Walter Michaels recovered the ball, but official Charlie Berry ruled it an incomplete pass.

That set the stage for a memorable fourth-quarter field-goal attempt by Pat Summerall, who went on to become the football play-by-play announcer for CBS-TV. Snow had covered the field markings and the flight of the ball couldn't be followed from the press box.

The kick was signaled good, and the length was listed as 49 yards, but that probably was just a guess. Summerall had missed a 36-yard attempt a little earlier in the fourth quarter.

A deflated Browns team arrived back in Cleveland that night after the 13-10 loss. The coin toss had been lost and the playoff game would be at Yankee Stadium.

The Giants were riding high after having defeated the Browns in the two regular-season games. The Giants won the playoff game, 10-0.

"Our hearts had been ripped from us by losing to the Giants

that way [on the official's ruling]," Paul Brown wrote in his book *PB: The Paul Brown Story*. "There was a hollow feeling in all of us having to prepare for another game in New York that shouldn't have been played."

The Giants went on to lose to the Colts in the NFL's first sudden-death overtime game. That was the game many observers believe started pro football's great surge in popularity.

Jim Brown well remembers the 1958 games, but doesn't recall much of the one at Yankee Stadium the next year. He was kicked in the head in the first half, couldn't remember the plays and had to leave the field because of an injury for the only time in his nine years.

Still groggy, he returned for some second-half action, but the Browns lost, 48-7. After the game, his face was puffed up.

Brown also has reason to remember the Concourse Plaza Hotel in the Bronx, where the team stayed on early visits. It was there that he was introduced to the media after being drafted for the 1957 season.

In the early 1960s, an elevator in the Concourse dropped free flight about five floors with Brown and several other players aboard.

The next season, the Browns moved their New York quarters to Manhattan.

# Cowboys Were at the Stadium the Day Ruby Shot Oswald

MY FIRST CONTACT WITH Dallas—the city, not the team—came in 1954 when several groups were working feverishly to snare a National Football League franchise.

The Browns and the Detroit Lions were booked into the Cotton Bowl for an exhibition. With Bobby Layne and Doak Walker, two Texas college football heroes, in the lineup and Texan Buddy Parker as coach, the Lions quickly became the "home" team.

Both squads attended a welcoming luncheon sponsored by the game committee. The master of ceremonies made no attempt to be neutral as he talked about the game and "our boys"—Layne, Walker and Parker. After about 15 minutes of accolades for the Lions, he introduced coach Paul Brown.

Noting that Dallas was experiencing water problems and was considering putting in a pipeline from the Gulf of Mexico, Brown suggested: "If our toastmaster can suck in as well as he blows out, put him to work on one end of that pipeline. You won't need any pumps."

Brown got a standing ovation—but only from his own players.

My first experience of racism in football occurred on this visit. The Browns' roster included such black standouts as Marion Motley, Bill Willis and Len Ford. But these future Hall of Famers could not eat or sleep at the hotel where their teammates were staying.

They would practice with the team each day during the week-long stay and then depart for homes of black families to spend the night. I don't remember any complaints, however.

For one thing, they got out from under Brown's thumb. And also away from the usual 11 p.m. road curfew.

After a week of some 100-degree heat, the night of the game arrived. It was to be a crucial test for Burrell Shields, a fine running back at John Carroll University who was being tested as a cornerback.

Layne had no mercy on the rookie. The Lions chewed up the Browns in general and Shields in particular, 56-31. Shields was gone the next week, but did catch on with the Baltimore Colts.

Six years later Dallas did get its own team. And a few seasons later, the Cowboys were scheduled to play at the Stadium the Sunday after that sad Friday in November 1963 when John F. Kennedy was assassinated.

For 24 hours, it was a guessing game if any NFL games would be played or if the Cowboys could even get out of Love Field, the Dallas-Fort Worth airport, that had been closed to all traffic.

The games, of course, were very secondary, but Commissioner Pete Rozelle made the decision that it would be business as usual. "It's a decision I regret very much," he said when he retired.

The Cowboys had lost to the Browns, 41-24, earlier that season and Cleveland beat them again, 27-17. Some 55,096 left their television sets to go to the Stadium and probably missed the slaying of Lee Harvey Oswald, Kennedy's alleged killer, by Jack Ruby on television shortly before kickoff.

Jim Brown remembers the Cowboys and the Cotton Bowl well. That was the scene of some of his longest runs and for one of his most dramatic—if shortest—touchdown runs in 1965, his final season.

Joan Ryan, who contributed a column to the *Plain Dealer* called Back Seat Brown through some of the seasons her husband, Frank, quarterbacked the team, wrote of the play:

"He swung around left end and was met by a group of bloodthirsty tacklers. He pushed off their grasping hands, lost his balance, went down on one hand, but somehow righted himself. With a couple of staggering steps, he regained his balance, spun off still another defender and skimmed into the end zone for 6 points, a determined effort."

Brown, now living in Los Angeles, was asked if he remembered that moment. "I remember that I liked it and that Blanton [coach Blanton Collier] liked it," he said. "It was more than the run, it was the situation in the game. There were other longer runs that gave me a lot of satisfaction, but I guess that one impressed some people, because I still see a rerun of it occasionally on television."

The Cowboys aren't the oldest rival of the Browns by any means. But the two clubs faced each other twice a year for a number of seasons after Dallas entered the NFL as an expansion team in 1960. With Paul Brown and Collier as coaches, the Browns won the first dozen meetings, but the Cowboys became more formidable as "America's Team."

# No Browns Loss Hurt as Much as 'The Drive'

OBJECTIVITY IS A GOAL worth striving for by any self-respecting reporter. It isn't always easy, though.

I discovered this fact soon after joining the *Plain Dealer* sports department in 1946. I am a John Carroll University graduate and spent some time there as director of public relations before joining this newspaper.

My first assignment in sports was to cover the local colleges—Baldwin-Wallace, Case Tech, Western Reserve and, of course, Carroll. My attachment to the Blue Streaks still was strong.

But I was determined to maintain that objectivity. And as I remember, many times I leaned over backward to make sure I didn't favor my alma mater.

The situation is somewhat different when covering the Browns, Indians or Cavaliers. You can't be a rooter in your writing, but most of the beat people want to see the team win.

For one thing, it makes the job more fun. Winning makes for a more pleasant relationship with the front office, the coaches and the players.

It really hasn't been difficult to maintain this posture over the years for most Browns games. But I must admit that on a few occasions I became a strong rooter by heart if not by mind. The visit by the Denver Broncos to the Stadium on Sunday afternoon brings this to the fore as I recall The Drive of 1987.

I had an intense desire to see the Browns win that playoff game against the Broncos at the end of the 1986 season and go to the Super Bowl. It would have been such a fitting climax to a spectacular year, one of the most exciting for coverage I ever experienced.

I was going to the Super Bowl anyway and having the Browns in the game would have involved much extra work. It would have been well worth it though to see the reaction of the city and Browns fans who rank with the top in the NFL.

As most present followers of the Browns will recall, the home team took the lead late in the fourth quarter. Bernie Kosar, in his second year with the club, passed to Brian Brennan for the go-ahead touchdown.

I watched that play from the press box. Brennan caught the ball at about the Denver 20-yard line on the 48-yard score. As I recall the pass was a trifle underthrown and Brennan moved back and to the inside to catch the ball. He was being covered by safety Dennis Smith.

"I was in good position," Smith said later in the dressing room. "Brennan reacted first. Then when I went to cut back inside, my feet got tangled up.

"I still managed to get a finger on the ball, but Brennan stuck with it and caught it. There really was no excuse for me not to make the play."

The extra point by Mark Moseley was my signal to start for the locker room. I took my customary route to the field, the elevator to the ground floor and then through the first-base dugout to the field.

Moseley had just kicked off with the wind at his back when I came out of the dugout. A gust seemed to lift the ball as it was coming toward the closed part of the Stadium and Denver's Ken Bell misplayed it. After some scrambling around, the Broncos got the ball on their 2-yard line.

Standing behind their offense as John Elway started to bark some signals, I looked downfield. The Browns' goal posts seemed miles away and the clock near the bleachers showed only 5:32 remaining. It looked like a sure Cleveland victory.

The wind blowing in my face was cold, but it didn't bother me. I was warm thinking of all the joy this victory was going to bring to so many people.

The Super Bowl was Marty Schottenheimer's obsession each season he was in Cleveland as coach. Browns President Art Modell would be fulfilled. He had been waiting since 1964. I was happy for some of the players who had felt all season that this was their year . . . and happy for the fans.

I couldn't hear it, but Elway seemed to say something as the Broncos huddled. Later in the visitors dressing room, somebody said that the quarterback smiled that toothy grin and said, "If we work hard, good things will happen."

Not exactly a Churchillian phrase.

Offensive lineman Keith Bishop is supposed to have told his teammates, "We've got them where we want them."

He probably stole it from Gen. Custer, but it proved to be true for Elway. He used up all but 37 seconds of the clock before finding Mark Jackson in the end zone from 5 yards. Jackson made a diving catch for the touchdown. Rich Karlis tied the score, 20-20, with the extra point.

Those scores completely deflated the crowd, the Browns and this writer. Even though the Browns won the toss and got the football in overtime, I was sure they were finished. The momentum had swung swiftly to the Broncos.

I had to rearrange my thinking in the short time it took for the Browns to go three and out and for the Broncos to move into position for Karlis' 33-yard winning field goal. The Denver locker room became my assignment and it wasn't easy to listen to the sounds of triumph—although the Broncos were gracious winners.

Linebacker Karl Mecklenburg put The Drive in perspective. "Cleveland was playing a prevent defense and our offense just didn't make any mistakes," he said."

A sad Schottenheimer was just about ready to leave the Browns' quarters when I stopped in.

"We'll be back again next year," he said. "I assure you of that."

The coach was right. They were back the next year and lost

at Denver in the AFC title game. And the Browns were back at Mile High Stadium in January 1990, only to get the same result, another defeat under a different coach, Bud Carson.

In many years of Browns watching, there have been tough losses as well as great victories. But I don't think there was a more difficult defeat to watch or a harder story to write than that one on Jan. 11, 1987.

It just points up the fact that a writer never should lose his objectivity.

# In 1965, It Really Was a 'Road' Loss

THE BROWNS' LAST NFL title game was against Green Bay in 1965. It might be labeled a championship chance that "slipped" away.

Maybe it was faulty motel booking that brought on the defeat. The team was housed the two nights before the game in Appleton, Wis., some 30 miles from Lambeau Field. That's a considerable distance, considering Green Bay's capricious weather in January.

The Browns were defending their 1964 NFL championship after an 11-3 season under coach Blanton Collier. They had scored fewer points and had allowed more than the previous season, perhaps the sign of an aging squad. But they had won six of their last seven games to finish the season with a flourish and win the Eastern Conference.

Collier's team had two weeks to get ready for either Green Bay or Baltimore. Those two clubs tied in the Western Conference and met in a playoff. That was the game in which the Colts had lost quarterbacks John Unitas and Gary Cuozzo and turned over the position to Clevelander Tom Matte. He went to work with plays attached to a wrist band and played well but saw his team lose in overtime, 13-10.

As they began serious preparation for the game against the Packers, the Browns had their own quarterback scare. Frank Ryan was hospitalized with a stomach virus.

However, Ryan was back at practice at Don Fleming Field on the Western Reserve University campus on Thursday and the team had a spirited workout.

The Browns flew to Green Bay on New Year's Eve and went immediately to the Holiday Inn in Appleton. It quickly learned that the paper-producing town had gained a minimum of fame as the site of Lawrence College and the birthplace of Senator Joseph McCarthy.

The squad probably had its most quiet New Year's Eve ever. The next day both teams worked out on a practice area next to Lambeau Field on a bright, sunny day with the thermometer reaching into the mid-20s.

The pre-game party for the NFL brass and the media was held at the Oneida Golf and Riding Club in Green Bay. The late Vince Lombardi, coach of the Packers, played golf there.

Lombardi was in a genial mood as he greeted friends. I had written a column a few days earlier suggesting he was on his way to the Pro Football Hall of Fame. He spotted me across the room and came over to give his personal thanks. We had become friends while taking daily strolls at the NFL meetings.

It was a pleasant starlit ride back to Appleton after the party. But the weather changed before dawn. First it was rain, then ice and finally snow.

The Browns' buses were on the road to Green Bay early, but it was a long, scary run. They slipped and slid and came close to accidents on several occasions. The players were thinking about survival rather than the game.

It was a late arrival at Lambeau Field, which had acquired that name a few months earlier in honor of former Packers coach Earl (Curly) Lambeau. And it was hurry-up all the way to the kickoff as workers shoveled snow from the stands.

The game was close for a half. A 28-yard field goal by Lou Groza left the Browns down, 13-12, at the intermission. But the Packers took charge in the third quarter and the Browns didn't score again. The final score was 23-12.

Jim Brown was held to 50 yards on 12 carries and seemed to have trouble with the slippery field. That was the last game for the Hall of Fame fullback, who retired the following summer to start his film career in England.

Ryan completed only 8 of 18 passes, one to end Gary Collins for a touchdown, and was intercepted twice.

It was a happy afternoon for the Packers and their fans, however. Three of the latter sat in midfield in a blizzard three hours after the game as this writer finished up his reports.

And Lombardi was a happy man. *New York Times* columnist Arthur Daley wrote the next day that the Packers had reached a "peak of excellence."

Little did he know that the Pack would go on to win the first two Super Bowls the next two winters.

But for this writer, the game will be remembered as one that might have been lost in the ice and snow on the road from Appleton to Green Bay even before the kickoff.

# Firing of Brown
# Was a Shock

IT'S AS IF SOMEONE knocked down the Terminal Tower.

That's the opinion one Cleveland sportswriter used when Art Modell fired Paul Brown. It was one of the biggest shocks in Cleveland sports history.

The firing of Brown came just after the Browns won their final game in 1962, defeating the San Francisco 49ers in Kezar Stadium.

That left the club with a 7-6-1 record, not a great campaign, but a winning one. There had been talk that Modell was upset with his coach and that there had been words on the plane returning from San Francisco.

This was all hearsay to most reporters. The Cleveland newspapers had gone on strike that November and none of the reporters on the daily papers made the trip to the west coast.

Brown invited my wife and me to spend New Year's Eve with him at Shaker Heights Country Club. He didn't talk much football that night and it seemed strange.

Mike Brown, his son, was there. As I recall there was another couple from the club. Mike had just finished at Dartmouth College, where he was a quarterback, and was working in the Browns administration.

New Year's Eve dinner was uneventful. I had to go to work the next day at a television station where I worked during the layoff and wanted to get some sleep.

The next Monday I was at work in the station's newsroom when the message came over the wire. Modell had fired Brown.

"I've made a decision," Modell told Brown. "You'll have to step down as coach and general manager."

Brown, now deceased, said later that he was stunned. "I really don't know what to say," he told Modell. "I have a contract with you for eight more years."

That contract was for $100,000 a season.

In his book *P.B. The Paul Brown Story*, Brown said Modell told him on the day he was fired that the team could never really be Modell's alone as long as Brown was around.

I was assigned by the station to go to the Stadium and interview Modell. He was nervous and excited but still had that sense of humor that has helped him so much over the years.

I asked him if there was any truth in the report that he would change the name to the "Modells." He looked startled, finally grinned and said, "There's not a chance we'll do that."

As I recall there wasn't as much talk about this change as there would be today. The papers didn't start publishing until the following April and the radio and TV stations soon went on to other sports pursuits.

There also weren't any strictly sports talk shows as we now have in Cleveland.

One magazine-type booklet came out with many of the sportswriters who concentrated on the Browns writing for it. It had one column that interviewed the fans and it was mixed, as might be expected with most of the people seeming to favor the better known Brown although his record had slipped since Modell purchased the club in March 1961.

I predicted in my story that Brown would be back in football. The only mystery was the time and place. It took longer than he expected but with the aid of Gov. Jim Rhodes and Modell, who approved the move, Brown took over the Bengals in 1967 and the team started playing in 1968.

The two patched up their differences over the years. In fact, as I told Brown on several occasions, his hiatus in La Jolla, Calif., did him a lot of good. He decided that he wanted to return and show Modell that he still could coach and he did that. He also spent much time with his ill wife, Katy.

Brown said in his book that Modell has gone "overboard to be nice to him." They talked at NFL meetings. Modell attended the Brown funeral in Massillon, and still is close to Brown's second wife, Mary.

So the passage of time usually heals most wounds.

# Browns Played Amid Tragic Events

THE BROWNS LOST TO Pittsburgh and St. Louis in their previous two games. That made it a 7-3 record with the Dallas Cowboys coming to town in that late November day in 1963.

It wasn't a bad day for November in Cleveland, just a bit chilly, as I drove out to League Park where the Browns were to practice. I was just coming into Lakewood when I turned on my car radio and got the bulletin.

"The president has been shot," the announcer said.

President John F. Kennedy was visiting Dallas that day. He was believed to have been gunned down by Lee Harvey Oswald, who days later was killed by Jack Ruby. I drove out to League Park where radio announcer Gib Shanley had passed along the word to Art Modell, who was in his third year as owner of the Browns. Modell decided not to tell the players until after practice.

Leo Murphy, now retired, was the trainer at the time. He had heard the radio bulletin and was stunned as he went about his work.

Practical questions arose. The radio report said the Dallas airport closed. The Cowboys were due to leave on Saturday for Sunday's game against the Browns at the Stadium.

Modell left the field and was in immediate touch with NFL Commissioner Pete Rozelle. The Browns boss thought all the games should be postponed.

I left his office to go downtown and get more information. Everybody at the *Plain Dealer* was in shock. No one could believe that President Kennedy was dead.

Gordon Cobbledick had just started his notes column, a Saturday feature in the paper. He sat at his desk immobile. Finally he gave up on the column.

"Tell Milt Ellis [the paper's deputy sports editor] there won't be a column tomorrow," he said. "I'm going home."

Hours later the word came over the Associated Press wire—the games would go on as scheduled.

Rozelle consulted with many people. He finally decided that would be the wish of the late president. In retrospect, the commissioner said if he had it to do over, the schedule would not been played.

My story was brief. It started with "The Browns will play the Dallas Cowboys as scheduled at the Stadium tomorrow, but football last night didn't seem very important to players, coaches, owners or reporters."

On Sunday I was getting ready to leave home when the word came from television—Ruby had shot Oswald in the basement of the Dallas police station.

Shanley got that news at his station. He heard the pinging noise of five bells from the news wire machine—the alert of a major news break.

From there he went to the Stadium where 55,096 people had shown up for the game. It was about the usual turnout for a game at that time.

The Cleveland dressing room was quiet. Several of the players were near tears. A police escort saw that the Dallas players got safely into their rooms although they were spit on and cursed. The crowd acted as though the team had something to do with the shootings.

The fans were unusually quiet during the game, many paying more attention to the radio reports from Dallas.

Dallas coach Tom Landry was asked how his team was affected by the national tragedy.

"We cut practice short when we heard the terrible news about President Kennedy," he said. "We couldn't have played a game

Friday or Saturday. Don't get me wrong. I'm not saying the outcome of the game was changed, but concentration for everybody,
the Browns and us, was difficult."

The same question was put to Browns coach Blanton Collier.

"I didn't talk to the players about it," he said. "There was no
need to talk. We all felt the same. Football is nothing compared
to things like this. The commissioner ruled we were to play and
we complied."

All this happened decades ago. It doesn't seem that long.

# THE GAME

# Media Remained Mum About Plum

IT WAS A DARK, chilly December day in 1957 and the Browns had just finished their first practice of the week at League Park for Sunday's National Football League championship game against the Lions in Detroit. Then disaster struck.

Quarterbacks Milt Plum and John Borton were tossing a football around as they headed for the locker room. Plum, scheduled to start against the Lions, put on a burst of speed to reach a pass and suddenly grabbed the back of his leg. To all observers, it was clear he had pulled a hamstring muscle, a common but usually sidelining injury.

"I don't know which one of us Paul Brown would have shot first if he had a gun handy," Borton said last week from his home in Massillon.

A few hours after Plum was injured, I received a call from the late Harold Sauerbrei, who was the team's publicity director and a former *Plain Dealer* sportswriter.

"Paul asked me to call you to ask you not to mention Milt being hurt," he said. "If the Lions find out, we won't have a chance. The other media people who saw Milt injure his leg have agreed not to say anything."

After a long debate with my conscience, I finally agreed to keep quiet.

Game time arrived in Detroit and a little guy named Tommy O'Connell started at quarterback for the Browns. But he wasn't fully recovered from a broken leg and it showed. Plum gave it a try, but had to limp off in the third quarter.

Borton, who had never fully recovered from a shoulder injury suffered while at Ohio State, finished the game, but without much success. Final score: Lions 59, Browns 14.

Brown quickly came up with his explanation of the loss in the crowded locker room. "Plum had a pulled hamstring," he announced to the surrounding media. "Everybody knew about it."

So I learned a lesson the hard way. That was the one and only time I didn't report what I saw as news from a practice or a game. Let the chips fall where they may.

Brown's request was unique. It hadn't happened before and didn't happen again as a string of coaches—Blanton Collier, Nick Skorich, Forrest Gregg, Dick Modzelewski, Sam Rutigliano, Marty Schottenheimer, Bud Carson, and Jim Shofner—followed Brown. Modzelewski and Shofner were interim coaches.

There was one occasion when I was asked not to watch a practice, but that was in Cincinnati. Bill (Tiger) Johnson was coach of the Bengals and having a rough season in 1978.

He didn't say anything one afternoon as I watched practice with the Browns—Paul, Mike and Pete—but the next morning, he called me over in the locker room with a request.

"I'm already in trouble with the fans down here," he said politely. "If they find out that I let a guy from Cleveland watch practice the week before a game with the Browns, they'll think I'm dumber than they thought before."

Johnson, one of the nice men in pro coaching and now working part time with the Bengals, was gone before the season was over.

Collier was a little suspicious just after he took the job. He asked me to come to his office one day and said: "I've been told to be careful what I say to you. I hear you are a friend of Paul Brown."

I told him that my coverage of the team would continue to be the same. Honest and objective, I hoped.

He soon had me out behind the offense with him at practice. Occasionally, he would point out something new the team was putting in for the next game. He never asked me not to report anything, but it's sort of an unwritten rule that new formations or special plays are not revealed.

Skorich, whom I found the easiest to work with of all the Browns coaches, did a superior job with inferior material. He had excellent relations with the media. He always started a season by having the media regulars with the team and their wives or girlfriends to his home in Brecksville, where his wife, Theresa, displayed her considerable culinary skills. That was an off-the-record session.

It also was a pleasure to work with Rutigliano. Outgoing and bright, he made the job of reporting easy.

Browns coach Bill Belichick told media they could watch practice, but not report what they see. If the rule was violated, the practices, Belichick said, would be closed to the media.

More and more people are involved in coverage now. The numbers could be one reason for a coach's paranoia about something aiding his opponents.

But in all my years writing, I never heard of a game being lost on a writer's slip or loose lips by the electronic media.

# NFL Draft Has Had Many Changes

THE NATIONAL FOOTBALL LEAGUE draft of 1950 was quite different from the present-day extravaganza.

NFL owners and coaches filed into the ballroom of the Bellevue-Stratford Hotel in Philadelphia, armed with a few football magazines and a couple of Manila folders with scouting reports.

Each of the 12 teams selected 30 college players before dawn. Selections weren't taken quite as seriously as they are now and some coaches spent considerable time at the nearest watering hole.

That was the way things were when the Browns moved into the NFL from the All-America Conference in 1950.

There have been major changes in four decades. Each of the 28 NFL clubs has such voluminous draft files, it would be a major move to transport them to a central headquarters. So teams do their selecting by telephone with a couple of representatives—equipment manager Ed Carroll and his aide, J.J. Miller, are the Browns' representatives—manning the phone at the New York City Marriott Marquis Hotel headquarters.

Drafts of long ago were held in November because of competition from the Canadian Football League. The CFL finished in November and immediately went after American collegians.

Paul Brown, the Browns' coach and general manager from 1946 through 1962, was one of the first to bring organization to the draft. Others soon followed until it evolved into the "science" that will be displayed Sunday and Monday.

Brown's first three first-round selections—running back Ken Carpenter and defensive backs Kenny Konz and Bert Rechichar—became starters. The next year, he chose Doug Atkins, a huge defensive tackle from Tennessee. Atkins eventually was elected to the Pro Football Hall of Fame, but mostly on his play with the Chicago Bears.

The Cleveland group returned to the Bellevue-Stratford in 1954 with high expectations. The team had a shot at getting the bonus pick.

The bonus pick, pushed for by the late NFL Commissioner Bert Bell, was given each year until every team received it so that the league's better clubs would get a blue-chip player at least every 12 years. The Browns won that first selection in the draft in a coin flip with Pittsburgh.

Brown was watched closely by the coaches at the other tables in the spacious ballroom. They knew he was looking for a quarterback to take over when Otto Graham retired.

Brown didn't hesitate in sending his choice to the podium. "The Browns take quarterback Bobby Garrett of Stanford," Bell announced.

But the pick proved Brown human.

When Garrett later visited Brown, vacationing in Florida, it was discovered that he stuttered. He needed the help of a Stanford teammate, not a pro prospect, to get the signals out. Garrett never played in a regular-season game for the Browns.

Three years later, Brown discovered that sometimes luck is better than skill at draft meetings.

Brown still was looking for a quarterback after Graham's retirement after the 1955 season. He had his eye on Purdue's Len Dawson, from Alliance, O.

The Browns and Steelers were tied in the standings at that point in the season.

The Browns lost the coin flip. Pittsburgh selected Dawson. So Brown settled for a Syracuse running back named Jim Brown, who had had a great day against Colgate the previous Saturday.

The next year, the Browns picked Jim Shofner, a defensive back from Texas Christian. Little did anyone suspect that the draftee was later to become a Browns assistant coach, head coach, pro personnel director and an assistant coach with the Buffalo Bills.

Dividing the college crop when there were only 12 teams provided a wealth of talent and depth for all clubs. Low picks often came through, as was the case for the Browns with Ben Davis, a defensive back from Defiance College. He was the 17th player picked by the Browns in 1967, but became an outstanding performer.

As the NFL expanded, the number of players taken by each team was reduced gradually to 12.

The 1962 draft took place at the Chicago Sheraton and is remembered for the start of the rupture in relations between Paul Brown and team President Art Modell. Modell had found out the previous day from another club owner in Dallas, where the Browns had lost, 45-21, that Brown had traded running back Bobby Mitchell and a first-round pick to the Washington Redskins.

The Redskins drafted Ernie Davis, another Syracuse back, with the first choice in the entire draft and sent him to Cleveland. Davis had great potential, but was diagnosed with leukemia and never played for the Browns. He died in the spring of 1963, four months after Brown had been fired.

Just as they had a year ago, the Browns had the second pick in the draft in 1970. All-Pro wide receiver Paul Warfield, a first-round selection in 1964, was traded to the Miami Dolphins for their first-round pick.

That choice was used to take Mike Phipps of Purdue, who was not the franchise quarterback he was anticipated to be. Clarence Scott and Thom Darden, two good defensive backs, were acquired with first-round picks in 1971 and 1972.

Linebacker Clay Matthews from Southern Cal, stayed with the team 14 years, and receiver Ozzie Newsome of Alabama were the prize picks of the 1970s. They were first-round picks in 1978, with the Browns taking Matthews first.

In the 1980s, there was a decline in the team's success in the draft. Talented players were picked, but running back Charles

White and linebacker Chip Banks had drug problems, and safety Don Rogers died from drug use.

In 1984, the Browns acquired fullback Kevin Mack and linebacker Mike Johnson in a supplemental draft of players from the U.S. Football League, and in 1985 the Browns picked quarterback Bernie Kosar in the supplemental draft.

But after that drafting success, the Browns faltered again with the selections of linebackers Mike Junkin (1987) and Clifford Charlton (1988).

The jury still is out on the No. 1 pick of 1989, running back Eric Metcalf, but Leroy Hoard, the team's first choice in the 1990 draft (45th pick overall) had a good 1991.

The draft isn't that different from going to the race track. Picking winners is never easy.

# The Year Sports Lost Its Innocence

THE YEAR WAS 1964. Cleveland's Jim Brown, with his blend of brute speed and power, had perfected the end sweep and taken the National Football League by storm with the play. It was The Championship Year.

It was 1964 and a gimpy-legged fellow by the name of Joe Namath came out of the University of Alabama looking for a job. He found one in the American Football League. And a place in the sport's history for negotiating the biggest contract ever—$427,000—and for having the first agent, a dealmaker named, appropriately enough, Mike Bite. Bite's slice of the deal, $30,000, was even paid by the New York Jets. Unheard of.

It was 1964. The year sports lost its innocence.

I blame it on Joe Namath. Broadway Joe made more money playing professional football than anyone had made before. He got a guaranteed salary of $307,000 a year and a Lincoln Continental. Three of his relatives were hired as scouts for three seasons at $10,000 a year.

The sports world was suddenly a field of dollar signs. Dealmakers were coaching baseball, basketball and football players in the fine art of the contract. Win, lose, draw, injured or not, everyone wanted to have a guaranteed salary because Namath had one. Five years after he signed his deal with the Jets, he was on the cover of *Sports Illustrated* carping about having to choose between his shady New York nightclub, Bachelors III, and a career in the NFL. The headline was "Namath Weeps."

Twenty-four years after Namath chose to make a few more passes—football, that is—I'm not exactly weeping over the state of the game, but I see that we have gotten what we paid for.

If it's true nobody cares about history, least of all football fans, then maybe I'm wasting my breath looking back and wondering where it all went wrong. But I've covered sports, mainly football, for 51 years in Cleveland. I go back to the year Paul Brown signed his first player to the Browns of the All-American Football Conference in 1946. I've seen the greats come and go and prove to be not so great after all. I've seen fan loyalty build to a frenzy and then ebb to indifference. I haven't seen it all—who wants to?— but what I have seen is a steady erosion of the sports world from a time when the athletes were young, eager and prideful to a day when dollars speak the loudest, fan loyalties are in a state of flux, and relations between the media and the sports world are fraught with mutual distrust.

Not long ago my daughter, Allie, found herself in an elevator with her husband and then-Browns quarterback Bernie Kosar. Her husband stepped right up and introduced himself and his wife, noting that Allie was my daughter. Kosar shook hands all around.

"I know Chuck, he's a nice guy. But don't tell him I said that," Kosar said as he stepped off the elevator.

Kosar was probably kidding, but the story is indicative of how relations between the media and players has changed. The players don't want anyone to know they are on good terms with sportswriters, fearful that that information might harm their relationship with other players or their fans.

Peek behind that curtain, though, and what you see is a world of business and commerce. The world of professional sports today is about money. And winning teams make money. So whatever it costs, right?

But money has robbed teams and owners of any sense of loyalty players might have once felt. And it's the fans who have suffered for it. They're reluctant to give allegiance to a player who may be gone tomorrow—players who are able to change teams the way fans change their socks. Twenty-four hours after Kosar was unceremoniously cut by the Browns, he announced, "I'm a Dallas Cowboy now." Period. It's hard to believe that Bob Feller, probably the greatest pitcher baseball has produced, remained with one team, the Indians, throughout his career.

History buffs, remember Brian Sipe? He came from San Diego State in 1974, beginning his 10-year career with the Browns for $12,000 annually. But like Namath, he went to the highest bidder as soon as he had a chance. In 1984, the New Jersey Generals of the World Football League paid $2.2 million over three years for his services.

Today, he seldom watches the game that made him a millionaire.

"My days with the Browns were fun and I really liked Cleveland, but I know this football is a business and I didn't regret moving on," he says.

"Donald Trump [owner of the Generals] was very honest with me. He paid off the third year of my contract even though I didn't play because I had a sore shoulder."

It's not as if money were anything new to the world of sports. Legendary Browns coach Paul Brown used to tell his players they were going on a "business trip" as they readied for an out-of-town game. What has changed is the sheer amount of money that supercharges the world of professional sports. Today, athletes can afford to get "bored" as Michael Jordan recently did.

But when the money got as big as Namath was cocky, the character of the sporting world changed in ways both small and large: Disagreements were no longer settled man-to-man, and agents were suddenly a growth industry.

I recall a day in the early '50s when I talked to Len Ford, a giant of a Browns player at 6 feet 6, boasting the weight of a young bull elephant. He was not only talented on the field: He also was a team leader.

I had written a story about one of Ford's teammates who had just joined the Browns. This player was unusual because he didn't have a college degree, but coach Brown, who was always looking for an edge, thought he had one with this muscle-bound man. But the young man was less than eloquent.

The story I wrote for the *Plain Dealer* honestly reflected this player's inarticulateness. As soon as Ford saw that story he took me aside.

"I know he talks that way," Ford said, "but it really makes him look bad. You know this guy is going to have a struggle, so why not give him, and guys like him, a break?"

I told Ford I would think it over. I decided Ford was right and that I admired him for coming to me man-to-man to lodge his complaint. Today, that would never happen. The age of the agent and the "spokesperson" has just about made it impossible. Today, a story like that would make an enemy.

However, sportswriters have to step up and take some responsibility for deflowering the world of sports for its fans. Sportswriters today are looking hard at the players and the coaching staff. Their reporting reflects that. Because when you know how much money someone is earning for your Sunday afternoon of fun, it's a lot tougher to get romantic about it.

But you know what? The game's not as much fun anymore. Players and coaches are not very friendly. They are not as accessible as they once were.

John Madden used to say that no one could ruin the game of football. He was only partially right. Nothing can ruin it, but football has been hurt and we have only ourselves to blame. Fans want winners. If a team is winning, no matter what the sport, attendance goes up. Team owners think fans want wins, not heroes whose years with a team are followed and collected like fond memories. I wonder about that. Maybe if we were all honest with ourselves we'd see that we'd like to have both.

Otto Graham was one of those guys: a hero and a winner. In each of his 10 years with the Browns, beginning in 1946, Graham led his team to the championships. They won seven of those 10 times. "Poise, ball handling and leadership" was how coach

Brown described him. Brown forgot to mention that Graham could also play the violin as well as the French horn. And perhaps most important of all, Graham embodied the spirit of a true athlete: He played hard and honorably.

Graham earned $25,000 during his final season.

"They told me at the time I was the highest paid player," he told me recently. "I got a $3,000 raise to come back and play that final season."

That was in 1955. Graham took the Browns to the title game and beat the Los Angles Rams handily. When it was over, the crowd gave him a standing ovation.

Spin forward 38 years to 1993 and the sad tale of All-Pro running back Emmitt Smith and his contract negotiations with the Dallas Cowboys. Smith refused to play unless he got "Thurman Thomas money." Translation: He wanted a deal worth $4 million a season.

Smith's actions frustrated his teammates and the fans. Defensive end Charles Haley slammed his fist through the dressing-room wall to let go of his steam. Fans booed coach Jerry Jones and Smith. When a deal was finally reached, it was to pay Smith some $13.6 million over four years. No one should give either party in that contract deal a standing ovation. Football is an unselfish game, often played by selfish players who take the joy out of the contest, the joy of watching sheer athleticism win a game, when they demand ridiculously huge amounts of money for their favors.

There is no going back to the innocence of yesteryear. But I will miss my heroes.

I know football is an outlandishly commercial sport. Take, for example, the Super Bowl, in which the cost of a commercial is as newsy as the game itself. But I still love it. I love the brute force, the strategy and the occasional miracle. All the star players in the world can't help an offense as much as five journeyman linemen who work well together.

It is, after all, games that we are talking about here. Games that appeal to all of us to some degree or another. Games that make us proud of our city and our team. Games that offer an outlet for our frustrations, assuage our need for heroes, nurse our vanity occasionally, and give us a sense of community. Games that should be played with honor in mind rather than money.

Joe Namath may have robbed sports of its innocence, but maybe we all share the blame.

# NFL Doesn't Break
# for Christmas

THE 1955 TITLE GAME was on the day after Christmas.

The late Paul Brown, then Browns coach, had no choice of when he would leave for the West Coast. Commercial jetliners still were on the drawing board, and it took eight or nine hours, with maybe a fueling stop, to fly that far.

Bert Bell, then NFL commissioner, demanded that the clubs be in the area two days before the game. So the Browns had to show up in Pasadena, their training center, the day before Christmas.

Sports editor Gordon Cobbledick realized it was an unusual situation. He called me in and said someone else could go if I really thought I should spend Christmas with my family.

The group included my wife, Pat, and three children—Sharon, Alice and Michael. Patty and Frances had not yet arrived.

Pat and I talked it over and she, knowing how much I wanted to see that game, offered a compromise. We decided to have an early Christmas and then I would bring the kids and her a bonus present from California.

That suited me, and the kids, being too young to know what was going on, also were satisfied.

So I gave Cobbledick the decision and took off with the squad. It was a gloomy day in Cleveland, but we broke through the overcast after about 15 minutes.

We arrived safely at the Green Hotel right on time. People from the old folks home that then was part of the hotel greeted us with egg nog. A huge Christmas tree decorated the lobby.

The regular season had gone 9-2-1, with the Browns losing to Washington and Philadelphia and being tied by the New York Giants.

It was the second visit to California for the Browns that season. The other two games were exhibition losses to the San Francisco 49ers and the Los Angeles Rams.

Sid Gillman was coach of the Rams, and Brown never cared too much for him. I remember waiting in the bus for the last few players after the preseason defeat.

Brown was seated in his usual first seat on the right side, and Gillman stuck his head in the door. "Your team will be all right, Paul," he said in a sort of condescending manner. "Just wait and see."

Brown found one remedy on his return to the Hiram College training camp. Otto Graham had agreed to come back if all didn't go well, and the quarterback signed a contract for $25,000 a year—most in the league—to play a final season.

The Browns had two weeks to get ready for that title game. In scouting the Rams, Brown noted that the club looked vulnerable to a double-wing attack.

So on that day after Christmas in the Los Angeles Coliseum, he unleashed the new attack. Graham, playing his last game, also helped immensely.

The Browns jumped to an early lead with the quarterback passing and running superbly. When he was taken out by Brown with five minutes left and the Browns winning, 38-14, he received a standing ovation from the crowd of 86,695.

Gillman didn't come over that night to the airport bus even to wish a Merry Christmas or just to say goodbye.

And the next morning, Pat and the Heaton kids had an extra present to open.

# HALL OF
# FAMERS

# Jim Brown, 1971

JIM BROWN WAS ELECTED to the Pro Football Hall of Fame in 1971. That year will always be bright in the memory of my five children and myself.

My first wife—the former Pat Hurd—and I were planning to take in the Super Bowl in Miami. I would attend the vote for the Hall of Fame candidates as usual.

The entrance of Brown was not unexpected because his career finished in 1965 with the Browns. He was probably the best running back in National Football League history.

I came home from attending Mass and doing my usual running to find Pat at the kitchen table almost unconscious. She had a tremendous pain at the back of her head. I suspected right away that it was a brain aneurysm.

The symptoms were the same as I had heard a few weeks before when the secretary in the sport's department died from the same disease. Pat was rushed by ambulance to Fairview General Hospital where she was given a 50-50 chance of survival

The game to be played between the Dallas Cowboys and the Baltimore Colts didn't mean a thing. Neither did Brown's election to the Hall. Her death came quickly two days after the Colts 16-13 victory. And Brown had gone into the Hall without any problems.

Brown was named with a fine group of athletes and Vince Lombardi, the late, great coach of the Green Bay Packers and Washington Redskins. The Class of 1971 also included quarterbacks Y.A. Tittle and Norm Van Brocklin, defensive end Andy Robustelli, tackle Frank (Bruiser) Kinard and Bill Hewitt, the late end. Van Brocklin died in 1983.

"I am happy to have been selected," said Brown upon learning the committee's action. "I look back at my time in football as good years.

"I don't feel that football has exploited me. And the reverse is true. People have to realize that it is a business as well as a sport. If you have that understanding then everything is all right."

Jim was asked at the time about the influence of coaches on his life.

"Ed Walsh, my coach at Manhasset High School, probably had the biggest influence," he said. "Then there was the attorney, Kenny Malloy—who did so many things for me and steered me to Syracuse. All the coaches had some effect—Ben Schwartzwalder at Syracuse, Paul Brown, Blanton [Collier]. All influenced me in a positive way from the standpoint of coaching.

"He went with me right away, even though I hadn't played much in the college All Star game. That developed my confidence. He believed in me, felt that I had the talent. That was the key to my whole mental attitude."

Brown was asked about Collier, his last coach.

"Blanton gave me the last part of it," Brown recalled. "It was the satisfaction of full expression. I caught passes and was part of the entire game. That was a very satisfying part of my football."

Jim remembers that 1964 championship game as the big game of his football career.

"It wasn't a particularly great game personally but we won the championship and everyone contributed," he said. "It was a good feeling to know we had won the world title. It was soon after that I began to think of retiring. Everything else has to be sort of an anticlimax."

A little over six months later, Brown was officially inducted. He was presented by Malloy who recounted his football record while making the introduction.

Brown said he had a fantastic time during the parade as the fans cheered his ride in an open convertible down the main street of Canton.

'The people responded and made me feel wanted," he said. "It was all natural and spontaneous."

He also thanked his mother, who was there, noting how hard she worked when he was a small boy.

"I want to thank her because I never tell her," he said.

Brown concluded his remarks with "the arrogant, bad Jimmy Brown can be humble when he is given true love."

It's many years since those induction ceremonies, and Brown now is closer to his old team than he ever has been. He is at practice much of the time and is doing all in his power to help out in many ways.

He quit the team for a movie career. Now he lives in his home in Los Angeles and works against gangs (Amer-I-Can) and turmoil. And he still is doing his best to make this country a better one.

As for this writer, he too has rebounded from that tragic death. He remarried—to Cece Evers—some years later. Now his children are beyond the college years and have youngsters of their own.

# Lou Groza, 1974

IT WAS A DAMP, chilly day at Cleveland Stadium in December of 1950. It also was Christmas Eve and many of the football fans were about their last second shopping duties.

Just under 30,000 took time off from those affairs to watch the Browns play what may be the most exciting and important game in the history of the club. Every radio in town was tuned to the game and many times the number reported in attendance heard the dramatic finish.

Otto Graham had fumbled the ball a few minutes earlier and it seemed that the Cleveland dream of a National Football League title was gone. Paul Brown, the coach of that club, didn't give up.

As the disconsolate quarterback came off the field he got a lift. "We're going to win," said Paul. "We'll get another chance."

The Los Angeles Rams moved the ball briefly, but quickly had to punt. The Browns got the ball back with less than two minutes to play and 68 yards from the Los Angeles goal line.

Graham, on fire, started the march with a quarterback draw for 14 yards. Otto then completed three passes to bring the ball to the 11-yard line. Graham ran the ball once more to position it in the middle of the field.

Then Graham and the players not on the kicking team came running off the field, throwing their helmets in the air.

"Stop that," warned Paul Brown, but he too was confident that the kick would be made. It all was up to Lou Groza.

Groza moved back from his offensive tackle spot and Tommy James, a fine defensive back, lined up to take the ball from center. Lou did what he always had done under such circumstances. He squared his shoulders and did all the things he had been doing since his days back in Martins Ferry, O.

The ball went right through the uprights. It was all over for the

Rams but they went down fighting. Warren Lahr put the frosting on the cake with an interception of Norm van Brocklin's long pass intended for Bobby Boyd.

It wasn't until he got in the dressing room and was the center of celebration that Groza became nervous. "I never thought about missing on the field but as I began to dress I wondered what a miss would have done for all of us," the kicker said.

The score was 30-28 with Groza's kick providing the final three points.

Later that evening when he got home he recalled the early training in Martins Ferry where he was an all-state player in football and basketball and an honor student. As a senior, the football team tied Toledo Libby for the state honors and the basketball club beat Lakewood High School for the state title.

Lou, who soon was to answer to the name of "The Toe," started his kicking with an older relative on a field in Martins Ferry. He was just a retriever for kicks but began booting the ball back and became interested. He soon did kicking at Martins Ferry High School and in his senior year at Ohio State.

He was 26 years old and married Jackie Lou Robbins, a girl from home, the May before that famous boot. He knew Jackie for a long time, first as a school girl while he was a high school star.

His first date with her was an accident. She was working as a model in New York and his younger brother Alex was up there playing with the Kentucky basketball team. Alex had a date with Jackie but didn't feel well so Lou filled in—and for life.

Lou had gone to Ohio State on an athletic scholarship. Ernie Godfrey was freshmen coach and the two worked on kicking fundamentals.

Before that year—1943—was over, he was called up for service in the reserve corps. He was sent to Abilene, Texas, for basic training and then assigned to Brooks General Hospital in San Antonio.

One of his officers suggested that he apply for the A.S.T.P. (Army Service Training Program) and continue his college work.

That program was abandoned shortly thereafter, and he found himself a private in the infantry. He was sent to the Far East for some very unpleasant work using his hospital skills.

The war was grinding to a halt when Groza got a message from Brown. Paul was coach of the new Browns and wanted Lou as one of his players.

"I didn't know anything about the league but figured if it was good enough for P .B. it was good enough for me," Groza rationalized.

So in the summer of 1946, he reported to football training at Bowling Green State University. Primarily a place kicker his first two years, he won the tackle job in 1948 and held it until a back injury halted him in 1960.

He was helping out with the coaching when Art Modell talked to him in 1961 and persuaded him to return as a kicker. He had 21 years of Browns football.

He finished after making 1,349 points in the NFL and 259 points in the AAFC and one NFL touchdown.

He wisely started working in the insurance business while playing. He and Jackie have four grown children.

"It's been a great life," said Lou, "but the one thing in football I'll never forget is that field goal on Christmas Eve. What a Christmas present."

# Dante Lavelli, 1975

DANTE LAVELLI PROBABLY HAD more nicknames than any of the Browns now in the Pro Football Hall of Fame.

"Gluefingers" is his own favorite one applied by the late announcer Bob Neal when he was doing the Browns' games. Another tag is "Clutch" which came from a scouting report by the Pittsburgh Steelers.

It read that in the clutch the Browns always threw the football to Lavelli.

Paul Brown, Lavelli's coach throughout his pro career and his presenter at Canton, remembered another affectionate tag. It was one of the most frequently used by Otto Graham, the great passer over most of his pro years. The name was "Spumoni" and came from his Italian parentage.

Lavelli was the son of Angelo Lavelli, a lifelong blacksmith in Hudson, O. "Poppa" wanted his son to carry on the family business but Dante's life has been connected in some way with the game so much loved ever since he signed up for Brown's first team in 1946.

Lavelli was a crack running back at Hudson High School, where the field now is named in his honor. Soon after he joined Brown at Ohio State he was turned into a wide receiver.

The service called during his sophomore year and he was assigned to the infantry and can boast of being one of those "battered bastards of Bastogne." When he came out of the service be had a chance to play baseball with Detroit but decided to join Brown and his new team in the All American Conference.

Lavelli and the late Mac Speedie, who also went on to football stardom, were the least known of the ends at that first training camp at Bowling Green. Brown knew the pair, however, and kept seven ends—Alton Coppage of the Chicago Cardinals, John Yonaker, a Notre Dame All American; John Rokiskey, All American from Duquesne; George Young, a player for Brown and Great Lakes Pinky Harrington of Marquette and Lavelli and Speedie.

Lavelli admits being plenty scared when he reported to camp and looked over the roster. But Yonakor dropped a first game pass in front of the Browns' bench and Lavelli replaced him. It was a move that proved to be permanent.

In Lavelli's first year with the Browns—1946—he caught 40 passes for 643 yards. He concluded that season by catching the winning pass in the 14-9 victory over the New York Yankees in the All America title game.

He was all league his first two seasons and earned the same honor in 1951 and 1953 when the Browns played in the National Football League. During his 11 years with the Browns from '46 to 1955 he caught 386 passes for 6,488 yards and 62 touchdowns.

Lavelli, who played at six feet and 190 pounds, caught a then-record 11 passes in the Browns' first NFL Championship game in 1950. Two of those were for touchdowns as the Browns won the game 30-28 on Lou Groza's late field goal.

During six title games in the NFL, Lavelli caught 24 passes for 340 yards.

The old white leather helmet he wore with the early Browns is still in his possession after being gone for a number of years. Joseph M. Koral and his young son, Tim, were part of the joyous mob milling around the players getting a victory rid off the field after the first NFL title.

Lavelli dropped the head gear during the excitement and Koral picked it up and took it home as a souvenir.

Dante was delighted to have it returned years later when he was elected to the Hall of Fame. "I kept it around the house for a while and now have sent it to the Hall," Dante said. "It is the only piece of equipment I have left from that game."

He received a note from Graham congratulating him on reaching the Hall. "I've heard a lot from my former teammates and old friends since the news was announced," Graham wrote in 1975.

"It's a reminder of the good old days. We really had a lot of fun."

It was in 1975 that films of Lavelli catching the football were used extensively in the Browns training camp at Kent.

"Dante was blessed with very good hands," Blanton Collier, the former Browns' late coach, used to say. "He also did the things a good receiver must do. He looked the ball right into his hands.

"Watch the film and you can see his head bobbing down as be looks the ball into his hands.

"He also had great confidence in his ability to catch the football. He'd come off the field and I'd ask him if he could do this or that. He never said he couldn't. He felt be could beat anybody any time."

Lavelli finished his work on his degree at Ohio State in the off seasons from football. He got that degree in 1949, the same year he married the former Joy Wright of Brecksville. The Lavellis have three grown children—Lucy, Edward and Lisa.

The former receiver has been busy in many facets of football and business. He has been an assistant coach with the Browns, an assistant with the College All Stars when Graham tutored the team and started the players' union, and also worked for the Chicago Bears as a scout. He also has invested in a health club, a golf course, a bowling alley and several other Cleveland enterprises.

Lavelli suffered a heart attack while chopping wood in 1976 but recovered nicely from it. He goes to the Hall of Fame each year for induction ceremonies, takes in all the Browns games, plays in a lot of golf tournaments and tries to take in all the Super Bowls.

Football has been good to Dante Lavelli over the years but he also has been good for the game.

# Bill Willis, 1977

BILL WILLIS WAS COACHING at Eastern Kentucky State College in 1945, having finished up at Ohio State, but he decided that he would like to play some more football.

He joined the Browns at their Bowling Green training camp and was welcomed by Brown. When he signed a contract, he became the first black player in the All America Conference.

Willis was a tackle at Ohio State where he won all types of honors. He was shifted to guard with the Browns because of his size—6'-2" and 210 pounds.

Teaming with Lin Houston, who also played at Ohio State, he promptly made the team although somewhat hampered by varicose veins which had required surgery. Before taking the job at Kentucky, he was voted the most outstanding player in the College All-Star game.

Willis was the quickest man off the ball, as he quickly demonstrated at training camp and as Brown already knew from his days at Ohio State. This speed made up for the lack of Willis' bulk, and he played with the Browns from the beginning year of 1946 through 1949 and stayed with the club during its first three years in the National Football League.

"It was a lot of fun playing all those years," said Willis. "They were a great bunch of guys and I have many wonderful memories."

Thinking back over the years, he remembers running down Chu Chu Roberts of the New York Giants in a playoff game and, of course, playing In the victory over the Philadelphia Eagles in the team's official debut in the NFL.

"The games and events sort of crowd together now, but those two things stand out," he said. "With Roberts the ball was about midfield when he broke free. I took off after him and tackled him about the seven-yard line. Then our defense came up with one of its famous goal line stands and they didn't score.

"The entire game against Philadelphia was great. We were as ready any team can be for that game. It was a tremendous feeling to know we had beaten the champs of football."

Willis was one of the best liked and most popular players on the Browns squad. He was a hard worker at practice but in the locker room he kept teammates loose with tales from his coaching year at Kentucky.

The players went both ways in those days and it was as a middle guard that Willis is often remembered.

Ed McKeever, coach of the Chicago team in the All America Conference, made it his business to study Willis and his performance as a middle guard.

"We studied the pictures of all the games and found that Bill usually followed a set pattern under certain conditions," McKeever said. "So we knew what to expect at times during the games. But it didn't do us any good. There is no way to beat Bill."

Told of McKeever's statement about his study, Willis was stopped at least momentarily. "I have no idea what he was thinking about," Willis said. "There is only one routine move for me and that's on my first defensive play. I like to see how strong my opponent is.

"Then I like to make contact with the opposing quarterback early, just to let him know I'm in the game."

Willis remembers that he felt more at home at guard. "I made many more tackles at guard than I did at tackle," he recalled.

"I just wasn't big enough to play tackle in pro football," he said. "In college it was all right even though I occasionally went up against a much heavier player. That didn't bother me because they usually were slow and clumsy. But here it's different. Big men are fast and agile. That added weight is too much of a handicap for me."

He was a dash man in track at Ohio State and his speed was a primary asset in football. He often would get by his man and to the quarterback before a handoff was made.

After eight seasons with the Browns, Willis decided he had enough football. So he accepted a post under John Nagy, then the city recreation commissioner. The yearly salary in his new job was $6,570.

"I wouldn't trade anything for my happy associations with the Browns," he stated upon retiring. "But this is the type of work I want to do, working with kids."

Willis is the father of three boys—Bill, Jr., Clement and Dan. All are grown now. His Wife, Odessa, still travels with him as he visits about the state in the role of a Hall of Fame athlete.

# Bobby Mitchell, 1983

THE SEASON OF 1961 was one of decision for Paul Brown and his football team. No championships had come in four years and the coach knew that it would lake a bold move to get him over the top in the National Football League.

So he made what proved to be a very unlucky one. He traded Bobby Mitchell, a fleet, high-scoring back to the Washington Redskins for the teams' first pick in the draft.

Brown knew of Mitchell's value to the Browns, but he also had seen Green Bay's domination of the game with two big backs—Jim Taylor and Paul Hornung. The swap was made at the 1961 draft held in Chicago and was one of the worst kept secrets in the NFL.

The Browns defeated the Dallas Cowboys, 38-17 in the Cotton Bowl and then headed north to the draft meetings. The annual lottery was held early that year so the American Football League, which already had drafted, wouldn't get too big a start at signing players.

The Browns had two first round selections. They used the first to get end Gary Collins of Maryland. They used the second to take Leroy Jackson in the draft and traded the Western Illinois back and a player to be named later to the Redskins for the rights to Ernie Davis.

The Davis story is well known. He learned he had leukemia at the College All Star game and never played for the Browns. He died from that disease in the spring of 1963.

Mitchell never was told directly by Brown of the deal. Two games remained on the team's schedule—a loss to the Chicago Cardinals and a tie with the New York Giants—before the season ended.

Mitchell was in training with his national guard unit but was given weekends off to play. He would come in on Saturdays, get the offense from Brown and be ready on Sunday.

"There were all kinds of rumors at camp about what was happening," Mitchell recalled. "John Paluck, a Washington player. was in the military, too, and he kept hinting about what might be happening. I didn't think it could happen to me."

The final game that 1961 season was in New York. Bobby was there and ready to play but Brown used him little.

"The players kept wondering why I wasn't in the lineup," Mitchell remembered. "They figured we'd win if I played. I guess, maybe, Brown didn't want me to play and look good. That would make his deal with Washington not so good."

After the game, Brown saw Mitchell in the dressing room. He didn't mention the trade directly but said that sometimes in football there were things that you felt you had to do. Then he said goodbye.

Bobby had been happy in Cleveland. He didn't carry the ball as much as Jim Brown but the two had a friendly rivalry. Sometimes after work at the Hiram college training camp they would sprint against each other. They were just about even most of the time.

"Bobby ran so smoothly," Jim recalled. "I pounded the ground. He scarcely seemed to touch it"

Mitchell had some great days as a halfback with the Browns. The afternoon he remembers most was one when a special play had been designed for him.

"It was a quick pitch and we practiced it all week," he remembers. "The players kept kidding me. They told me I'd better make it work.

"Well game time came and I ran the kickoff back about 40 yards. I was in the lineup and in came the play. It was my special play.

"I still was out of breath from the kickoff play and thought 'why doesn't he wait?' But you know what happened—I ran for a touchdown. I think it was against the Eagles."

Mitchell liked it in Cleveland. He had just purchased a home there and his wife, Gwen, was busy getting acquainted with the neighbors. He and Gwen have two grown children, Robert, Jr. and Terri.

Gwen has her law degree and worked for the government in Washington.

"I was really sick at leaving Cleveland but it turned out to be a wonderful thing," he said recently. "Bill McPeak was the coach and he asked me what I thought about playing as a receiver. I told him that they had thought about it in Cleveland but Ray Renfro was there—a very good one—plus some other capable guys. So it wasn't done.

"I said I'd like to try it and he changed me. It proved to be a great move."

Mitchell got along very well with the people in Washington. He became very friendly with Edward Bennett William who was to run the club when George Preston Marshall became ill. He met Bobby Kennedy and they became friends. There were many others in the nation's capital with whom he became close.

The Redskins played Cleveland in 1962 in the second game of the season. Bobby scored the winning touchdown in the Skins 17-16 victory, and they won again in the second meeting in Washington.

"It turned out to be a beautiful deal for me," said Mitchell who went into the Pro Football Hall of Fame in 1983. "I retired as a player in 1969 and immediately joined their scouting staff."

This is his 37th NFL season and during the 33 years with the Skins he has been a player, director of scouting, assistant to the president and now is assistant general manager.

"You never know what is going to happen to you," Mitchell said. "I felt it was a dark day when I was traded. It proved to be one of the best days of my life."

# Paul Warfield, 1983

THE BROWNS HAD THE honor of having two of their players go into the Pro Football Hall of Fame in Canton, Ohio at the same time. Paul Warfield, who still lives in the Cleveland area, went in with the Browns' Bobby Mitchell and quarterback Sonny Jurgensen, linebacker Bobby Bell and coach Sid Gillman in 1983.

A soft-spoken, quiet man, Warfield was the most eloquent that day as he accepted the award. "This is the highlight of my career," he said. "It is the biggest thing to happen to me.

"I'm so proud to be in this class with such great individuals. I'll remember this forever and ever. I'm so happy to be taking my place in football history."

Capital University coach Gene Slaughter who tutored Warfield 20 years before at Warren Harding High School was there to make the presentation. "He is the greatest athlete I've ever seen and my hero of all time," the coach declared.

So was Woody Hayes, Warfield's coach at Ohio State University. Warfield gave tribute to his old football coach as "a man of great integrity, tremendous honesty and great compassion. First we were students, then players," he said.

Warfield earned that honor by playing football for the Browns from 1964-69 and again in 1976 and 1977. He spent the year of 1975 with Memphis of the World Football League after spending four years—1970-1974—with the Miami Dolphins. He was with the undefeated Miami team which won the Super Bowl and a perfect season of 17 straight games in 1972.

The Browns first draft pick, Warfield made his initial showing with the team at Lakewood High School in 1964. Blanton Collier gathered the troops for the only spring workout at Lakewood High School.

Warfield had been a fine defensive back with the Buckeyes and he was drafted with that position in mind. But Collier wanted a peek at him as a receiver. One look by Collier and Dub Jones, the coach of the offense, was enough. The defense never got him back.

The Browns had good quarterbacks in those seasons. There was Frank Ryan, Bill Nelsen and Brian Sipe.

"Ryan was as good as any quarterback in the league at that time," Warfield says. "I really respected Bill Nelsen and what he accomplished despite some physical problems. He knew how to get the ball to me the way I wanted it.

"Sipe was just learning when I returned to the Browns. You could tell right away that he had the competitive spirit and the desire to succeed that would make him a fine quarterback."

In 1970, Art Modell announced that Warfield had been traded to the Dolphins for that team's first draft choice, who turned out to be Mike Phipps of Purdue University.

Miami was not a passing team but he was acclaimed in that city and given a big pay raise. He never lost his Cleveland ties though, and still remembers coming back for a Monday night game in 1973. It Warfield's first Cleveland Stadium appearance since being traded.

"I remember when they called my name as a Miami starter," Warfield said. "The Stadium crowd burst into one of the loudest ovations I've ever heard in my life. They were cheering me and it must have lasted five minutes. It was one of the most profound experiences of my life. I remembered thinking that the Cleveland fans hadn't forgotten me."

Warfield became a free agent in 1975 and the World Football League made its offer. He took the one that landed him with the Memphis Southmen. That league folded up after one full season and part of another but his salary was paid. He then returned to the Browns for two more seasons. That made it a total of 14 seasons of pro football, a long time for a wide receiver.

He was married to Beverly in 1964 and they have enjoyed a

fine relationship over the years. They had known each other for a long time as schoolmates in Warren before marriage.

Paul has been in the Browns' front office in a variety of capacities and also worked in radio and television. In 1987, he left the team to join a former teammate with the Browns, Ernie Green, in business in Dayton. Recently, he entered into a partnership with some friends in Miami. Business includes selling T-shirts and other wearables with sports' team logos. He spends part time in Florida and does some other traveling. Bev, who has had an assortment of jobs since their marriage, is busy with several projects.

There are two children, Sonja and Malcolm.

Through his career in professional sports and in business, Warfield has learned at least one important thing. "If you treat people with respect, they will in turn treat you with mutual respect," he said.

# Mike McCormack, 1984

MIKE MCCORMACK MIGHT BE a retired insurance executive right now if it weren't for one of his teammates with the Browns. Following his departure from the Browns he was in the insurance business in Kansas City for three years.

Otto Graham, the Browns' quarterback in 1954 and 1955 when McCormack joined the team, had been given the job of coaching the College All Stars. In forming a staff. he remembered Mike as a bright, young player who had recently retired from football. So McCormack was persuaded to come back into football part time.

McCormack, who was in Canton a few weeks back as one of the returning class of 1984. recalled those days with the All Stars.

"It was fun to be in football again," he said of the two years with the Stars. "Lou Saban had asked me to join his staff at Buffalo after I left the Browns [1962], but I wasn't sure what I wanted to do.

"Then Otts got the part time job with the All Stars and I decided to go with him. I liked it and it didn't take much persuasion to join his staff when he became head coach of the Washington Redskins in 1966."

As the story goes, McCormack quit the Browns in 1962 because Paul Brown had been fired.

"That isn't exactly true," he said. "I had been playing football a long time. Ann was expecting another baby, and I wanted to be with her. I had missed the others because of training camp. After nine seasons with Cleveland, it just seemed the right time to leave."

The McCormacks now have four grown children, Michael, Tim, Molly and Collean.

During the time away from coaching Mike helped the Texas team of the American Football League move to Kansas City and become the Chiefs. But when Graham was given the job of coach of the Redskins, McCormack started his life's work in the National Football League.

At the present time he probably is the most experienced man in the NFL. From player, he went to assistant coach, to head coach, to general manager, to president and now to president of the Carolina Panthers, a team that will begin operating in the NFL in 1995.

McCormack came to the Browns in the 1954 deal with the Baltimore Colts. It was the largest and maybe the best ever made by Paul Brown.

The coach gave up 10 players, but in addition to McCormack, he received defensive tackle Don Colo and Tom Catlin, a linebacker. Both almost immediately became starters with Cleveland. Don Shula, later to become the famed coach in the NFL, also departed in the deal.

McCormack was the key man in the swap, however, even though he had a full year of army duty remaining. Brown lobbied for McCormack's entry into the Hall of Fame and called him "one of the very finest persons I ever coached."

Mike was an offensive tackle at the time of the trade but found himself projected as the man to fill Bill Willis' spot at middle guard. Willis, also in the Hall of Fame, had just retired at the end of the 1953 season.

McCormack made the move very successfully and led the defense to the 1954 NFL championship. He made a spectacular play in the title game, a defeat of the Detroit Lions.

"I'll never forget the play," Graham recalled. "Quarterback Bobby Layne was dropping back to throw a quick slant. Mike just reached across and took the ball right out of Layne's hands."

That play came early in the game and as a factor as the Browns went on to a 56-10 victory.

The next season—1955—Bob Gain returned from service and McCormack was shifted back to his natural position as offensive tackle.

"Mike did well at middle linebacker and could have played either spot." Brown said. "But his No.1 niche was offensive right tackle. He was an excellent pass protector but could also blow people out of there. He was a stabilizing factor throughout the period he played for us."

Mike McCormack was named to five Pro Bowls and to all-pro clubs of some type every season he played. His last Pro Bowl came after his final season in 1962.

Graham again sought out McCormack in 1966 when Otts became head coach of the Washington Redskins. McCormack was an assistant with the Redskins for 11 years also serving under the great Vince Lombardi, Bill Austin and George Allen. He also was head coach of the Baltimore Colts in 1980 and 1981 and head coach of the Philadelphia Eagles in 1973 through 1975. He rejoined Paul Brown as an assistant for the Cincinnati Bengals in 1976 through 1979.

He joined the Seattle Seahawks in 1982 as director of football operations and became president and general manager in 1983 and took over as president and director of operations of the Carolina team in 1991.

# Frank Gatski, 1985

FRANK GATSKI, ALWAYS ON the quiet side during his 11 years with the Browns and final season with the then NFL champion Detroit Lions, wanted to know if I had heard from the Browns' Otto Graham, the quarterback, and guard Abe Gibron of his playing days.

"I heard that Graham hadn't been feeling too well," he said. "Abe was my Hall of Fame presenter. He wasn't in the best of shape then."

Gibron was the leader of that fine Browns' offensive line and is now retired after many years as a player and coach. He did the honors for Gatski in Canton in perhaps the most famous class to enter the Hall.

Along with Gatski were quarterbacks Roger Staubach and Joe Namath, running back O.J. Simpson and Pete Rozelle, then the commissioner of the National Football League.

"I'm still a Browns' fan but watching them in person or on television isn't like playing the game," Gatski said. "I loved the game; playing it was fun."

Gatski had almost given up hope of getting into the shrine in Canton, but the selection committee for old timers cast their vote in 1985 and he made it.

"Getting in was the best feeling I've had since we hung it on the [Los Angeles] Rams in the first NFL title game," Garski declared. That was the Browns' victory in 1950 when they won 30-28 on Lou Groza's field goal.

"Deep down I thought I might have a chance of making the Hall," he continued. "Then I saw the list of all those great players and I wasn't too hopeful. This really is being on the top of the heap."

Gatski enjoys the feelings of being in the Hall, but never would have complained if he hadn't made it "Just playing all those years was enough for me," he recalled. "I felt if I made it okay, if I didn't okay.

"If I had it to do over, I'd do it the same. If I could still play another game, I'd put on my togs and run all the way to California."

Gatski wasn't as big as today's pro football figures go. He stood 6-3 and weighed 240 pounds. He had an ideal build for a center, however, with what was known as a high split. He had long legs and the quarterback could wait the snap of the ball standing up.

"The quarterback always had one less worry," Graham said. "No one was going to smash through the Gunner and mess up a play before it got started."

Paul Brown used to say that Gatski was the strongest man on that first Browns' team. "He had a rhythm for getting the ball back to the quarterback and that's more of a trick than one would think," the coach used to say. "Frank probably was one of the strongest men on the squad."

Gatski was living in Barrington, W. Va. when he agreed to his first contract with the Browns when Brown organized the club in 1945. He recalled that he hitchhiked from his home to try out for that first club.

"I signed for $3,000 a year," he remembers. "I wasn't sure what would happen and wanted to save the money. Even if I made the team I wouldn't have much money to spare."

That first squad included an experienced pro center in Mike Scarry. So the Gunner was a substitute for that initial season and part of the second. Then he took over the job and never missed a snap.

Garski said he remembers two game very well. The first was the initial one in the NFL when they opened against the defending champion Philadelphia Eagles.

"We were the upstarts from the All-America Conference," he said. "But we won. We used the forward pass so much that they kept calling us sandlotters. Then we played them again that season and didn't throw a pass but still beat them."

Durability was another trait of Gatski. He never missed a game, a practice or called a timeout during has career.

He was far younger in body than most men his years," Brown commented after his eighth of nine seasons "For many years we didn't even carry a backup center. The outdoor life he leads in the off season has taken care of that."

Said Gatski at the time, "You've got to be tough to play football."

And the Gunner indeed was a very tough man but also a very nice one.

# Leroy Kelly, 1994

LEROY KELLY IS A patient man. He also is very confident. He felt that he deserved to go in the Pro Football Hall of Fame and that the honor would eventually come to him.

He had to wait longer than anticipated but never lost faith in the selection committee. The night before the selection committee met in Atlanta, Ga. during Super Bowl week he didn't waver.

"I feel positive about it," he said from his home in Willingboro, N.J. "This is my time. You never know what goes on in other people's minds but I believe I contributed much to the success of the Browns."

"I'm pretty excited about my chances. I just hope the voters see it as I do."

Kelly had been a finalist several times in the past when he first became eligible after five years away from football He didn't quite make it and then it seemed that he had been forgotten.

The years passed quickly and he was a member of the old timers' group. His fate was up to a committee of five selectors who met in Canton, at the Hall in June of 1993.

Kelly had to be nominated by this group before his name could go before the regular selection committee. That action took place and then he was in the hands of the full committee for election.

I am a member of both committees and felt confident when we sat down in the Phoenix Room at Atlanta's Hyatt Regency Hotel I had had conversations with several members of the committee and most of the old timers agreed that Kelly should have made it many years earlier.

I made much the same presentation that I had several times in the past. This time I wrote out what I wanted to say so nothing would be forgotten. I also talked to several other committee members and asked them also to speak for Leroy. They all responded without hesitation.

Among the things I told the new members of the committee who hadn't seen Kelly play is that they had missed something very special. I thought his most telling statistic was the 90 touchdowns he scored.

Kelly had great drive, particularly in the red zone. Gene Hickerson, the Browns' fine guard of that era, called Kelly the best "going-in-to-score running back I've seen."

Hickerson saw evidence of greatness in this man from Morgan State in his first two seasons when Jim Brown was doing practically all the ball carrying. "Watching him as a kick returner I knew he had what it takes to be a great back," Hickerson said.

During his career of 10 seasons with the Browns, he played in 136 games. He was in a large measure responsible for the team going into the championship games in 1968 and 1969. He was a member of the special teams in the 1964 title bout and the next seasons when the Browns lost to the Green Bay Packers. Those were Jim Brown's final two seasons.

Kelly's credentials included 12,329 combined yards—7,724 rushing, 2,281 receiving. He led the league in rushing in 1967 (1,205 yards) and 1968 (1,239 yards), in scoring in 1968 with 120 points and in touchdowns in 1966 with 16 and in punt returns in 1965 with a 15.6-yard average.

Kelly's figures would have been even more impressive if he hadn't had Brown in front of him in 1964 and 1965. But he has no regrets.

"I'm proud of having been on the same team with Jim Brown," he said after the election. "That got me ready for things to come." Then he added with a grin, "I am thankful for him going into the movie business when he did."

Kelly took time at the Hall of Fame ceremonies and after his nomination to thank his ex-teammates. He knows that football is essentially a team game.

"I want to thank the guys I played with for all their help," he said. "Football is a team game. Nobody does it alone. A lot of people help you on every play."

Kelly also had to thank the late, great Buddy Young for his part in the Browns' eighth round selection. Young was a scout for the Baltimore Colts in those years and saw the signs of greatness in Kelly during his years at Morgan State.

Buddy found that the Colts weren't interested and he asked Browns' owner Art Modell to make Kelly a Cleveland choice when the eighth round of the draft came up. The Browns had Jim Brown at the height of his career but Modell decided to take a chance. It proved to be a stroke of genius when Jim retired after two years.

The back got along well with the other players and the media. He was quiet and friendly and reporters liked him.

Kelly remained a quiet, nice person during his years in retirement. He admitted his feeling that he somehow would eventually be in the Hall.

Now he has made that big jump to the place where only the great players in the game go. He was a very happy man in Canton as he accepted the honor and now is where he belongs—along with Jim Brown, Marion Motley and all those great Browns.

# POSTSCRIPT

# The All-Time Greatest
# Browns Team

THEY COME AND THEY go—owners, coaches, and players.

Good people make any good organization work. And the people involved with the Cleveland Browns over the years have been some of the best in pro football.

The team that first billed itself as "The Greatest Show in Football" has pretty much lived up to that tag through the parade of outstanding players who have worn the brown-and-orange colors so proudly.

Paul Brown knew what he wanted in a pro football team when, in 1946, he gathered players together at Bowling Green State University.

"We're going to be the New York Yankees of this game," he told the service-scarred veterans and pink-cheeked college seniors. "They are the best in baseball. We will be the best in pro football."

Brown received the green light from McBride, the taxicab and real-estate tycoon, to do just that. McBride knew nothing about football except that he was a Notre Dame subway alumnus. His pockets were deep, however, and he was willing to spend.

After the 1945 season, the Cleveland Rams abandoned the city for warmer climes. Team members took their National Football League championship rings with them. But the fans and the media had few regrets about the loss of a club that never captured the heart of the community.

In fact, Cleveland's Big Four college teams—Case Institute of Technology, Baldwin-Wallace College, John Carroll University and Western Reserve University—often attracted more fans than the Rams. And, of course, statewide football interest was centered on Ohio State University.

When the *Plain Dealer* sportswriter who covered the Buckeyes was asked to choose between covering the new Browns or the Scarlet and Gray, he chose the Big Ten power.

This was the Cleveland football scene in the fall of 1945, when I returned to the city after two years in the military. At the *Plain Dealer*, I soon became a member of the sports department and began covering the Browns and professional football.

I had a front-row seat from which to watch the growth of a football franchise. I had a perfect view of the parade of gifted— and not-so-gifted—athletes who stepped onto the field.

Some 600 athletes have made the regular Browns' squad since that first summer camp at Bowling Green. For me, most of them are more than just a name or a number in the team's press guide. So it was with alacrity that I undertook the assignment of picking the All-Time Greatest Cleveland Browns Football Team.

At first the task was easy. Otto Graham, Jim Brown, Lou Groza, Dante Lavelli, Mike McCormack, Marion Motley, Mac Speedie— the names jump out at you.

But how do the players rate against each other? Where are some positioned? Often, only a hairbreadth separated the first and second team choice.

So here are my picks. These are the best' players at their positions to play for the Browns.

## OFFENSE

*Quarterback*
### OTTO GRAHAM

The quarterback makes or breaks a pro football team. Paul Brown knows this, and he doesn't hesitate when asked about his most valuable player.

"Just look at the record," said Brown, 80, general manager of the Cincinnati Bengals, from his office at Riverfront Stadium.

Graham's record *is* impressive. He played in 10 championship games in his 10 seasons at the helm. His clubs won championships in all four years in the All American Conference and took three titles in his six years in the NFL.

Since he retired in 1955, after a 38-14 victory over the Los Angeles Rams at the Coliseum, the Browns have won just one NFL title—in 1964.

Most of Graham's records have been erased by his successors. But only Graham, maybe the greatest passer of all time, produced the championships.

Who would be my pick to back up Graham?

None other than Brian Sipe, who broke many of Graham's passing records. He beats out Frank Ryan, Bill Nelsen, Milt Plum and others.

*Fullback*

**JIM BROWN**

If Graham is the most important player to play for the Browns, then Jim Brown is a close second. Brown, the legendary No. 32, was a man on a mission when he arrived at the club's Hiram College training camp in the summer of 1957. He drove into the sleepy town in his fire-engine-red convertible after an all-night run from Chicago, where he had played only a so-so College All-Star Game the previous night.

There was silence in the Browns' dressing quarters when Brown stripped down, displaying his classic physique, which should have been captured in bronze and displayed in an art museum.

Paul Brown, eagerly awaiting the appearance of his first-round draft pick from Syracuse University, saw Jim run only a few plays at the morning workout. But he was so impressed that he told Brown after practice, "You're my fullback."

And that's the way it was every game for nine years before Jim Brown prematurely retired in the summer of 1966. He owned just about every NFL rushing record.

My second-team choice? Jim Brown pushed Marion Motley, a

Pro Football Hall of Famer and maybe the second-best pro full-back of all time, to that slot. Motley, a blockbuster runner and superb blocker, took it as a personal affront if Graham came off the field with any dirt on his uniform.

## Halfback
### LEROY KELLY

It's unfortunate that the brilliant Kelly, from Morgan State University in Maryland, had to spend several years of his pro career in Jim Brown's shadow. But he made a major impact in the NFL returning punts and kickoffs.

Kelly still holds the team record of nine consecutive games in which he scored touchdowns rushing. Only two players in NFL history, Lenny Moore of the Baltimore Colts and John Riggins of the Washington Redskins, have topped that.

Kelly was not widely known around the league when he took over for Jim Brown. But his coaches and teammates knew of his talent.

"We'll be just fine," said Dub Jones, the Browns' offensive coordinator, when Jim Brown retired. "We have Leroy. People don't realize how good Leroy is."

Kelly's backup? My choice is Bobby Mitchell, now in the Hall of Fame as a wide receiver, who was Jim Brown's sidekick before being traded to the Washington Redskins. He beats out Ernie Green, an underrated runner and blocker.

## Wide Receiver
### DANTE LAVELLI AND MAC SPEEDIE

At this position, the Browns have been particularly blessed. Lavelli and Speedie were the first tandem. Then came Paul Warfield, who also had some of his best days with the Miami Dolphins, and Gary Collins, the most valuable player in the 1964 NFL title victory.

Old-timers don't ask whether Lavelli *and* Speedie belong on the all-time team. No, the argument is which one was better.

Lavelli always thought he could catch the ball, and he did it very well in a crowd. When in distress, Graham would just listen for a high-pitched cry: "Otts! Otts!" Graham knew the voice was Lavelli's.

Speedie was a more selective receiver. He knew when he could get open and when he could beat his man. When he spoke, Graham listened.

Ray Renfro was another receiver of great talent. So was Dub Jones, who ran from a halfback spot. And longtime fans still remember the catches of Darrell (Pete) Brewster.

But my second-team receivers have to be Warfield and Collins.

## Tight End
### OZZIE NEWSOME

The Wizard is the team's greatest, and maybe the league's best, at this position. He surely will be enshrined in the Hall of Fame as soon as he is eligible.

Milt Morin is Newsome's backup at the position, but he probably played more at wide receiver. Morin was very good and a fine athlete, but he doesn't compare with Newsome.

## Center
### FRANK GATSKI

A member of Paul Brown's first team, Gatski finally received long-overdue recognition when he was elected to the Hall of Fame in 1985. He came out of Marshall College in West Virginia; and although he didn't left weights, he may have been the strongest man to play for the Browns.

The Gunner, as he was called, took over the center spot from Mike Scarry in 1948 and played for the Browns through 1956. He later spent one season (1957) with the NFL championship Detroit Lions.

Gatski's backup is Tom DeLeone, a more modern-era performer. He beats out John Morrow and Fred Hoaglin.

## *Guards*
### GENE HICKERSON AND JIM RAY SMITH

Hickerson may be forgotten as far as Hall of Fame voters are concerned, but he hasn't been forgotten by Cleveland fans who remember him leading sweeps for Jim Brown. Hickerson, still a Cleveland resident, played for 15 years and was a solid player until the day he retired.

Smith, a Texan with the look of an athlete—tall, blond and handsome—played the position as well as any lineman who wore the brown-and-orange.

Backing them up are John Wooten, now a coach for the Dallas Cowboys, and Abe Gibron. Wooten, Hickerson's running mate for years, also was a key blocker on Jim Brown's sweeps. Gibron was so fast off the ball that his teammates accused him of jumping offside. The officials, however, never thought so.

*Editor's note: The Hall of Fame voters finally remembered Hickerson in 2007.*

## *Tackles*
### LOU GROZA AND MIKE MCCORMACK

Groza is one of those two-position men on the squad—a tackle extraordinaire and place-kicker deluxe. The Toe probably is best known for his kicking—particularly the field goal that topped the Rams in the 1950 title game in Cleveland—but he always thought of himself as a tackle.

"I never forget that I was a lineman first," he said. "Kicking gave me longevity and fame, but I always considered myself a tackle."

And The Toe was good enough at that position to make the Pro Bowl nine times on the vote of his peers.

McCormack, now president of the Seattle Seahawks, was a superb lineman, a fine technician and, above all, a great team leader. He played some middle guard and did it well. But he really found his niche when he was moved to offensive tackle. One of Paul Brown's favorite players. he retired from the game in 1962, after Brown was fired by Art Modell.

Not too far behind Groza and McCormack are two other tackles of talent, skill and longevity—Doug Dieken and Dick Schafrath. This is a position where runner-ups would be first string on most squads.

## DEFENSE

And now comes the all-time defensive group. You make headlines with the offense, but the defense wins titles. And that's the way it was with the Browns, even in the days of Otto Graham and Jim Brown.

### *Ends*
#### LEN FORD AND PAUL WIGGIN

When the Los Angeles Dons franchise folded, the Browns participated in a special draft. Paul Brown, whose ability to judge talent has been one of his strengths, immediately tapped Len Ford.

Ford, 6-5 and 260 pounds, was the first of the true pass rushers. An All-American at the University of Michigan, Ford soon was on his way to the Hall of Fame.

Wiggin, in contrast, was only 6-3 and 245 pounds, but he was the complete player. He had talent and brains. He was a leader on and off the field, and he went on to coach.

Their backups are Bill Glass and Lyle Alzado. Glass, now an author and evangelist, was a team leader and one of the club's best pass rushers. Alzado, who came in a trade with Denver, also was a player and team leader.

### *Tackle*
#### BOB GAIN AND WALTER JOHNSON

Both players had long, illustrious careers. They were tremendously strong men, who were particularly effective against the rush.

Gain, out of the University of Kentucky, suffered a broken leg in the 1964 championship season but came back to play better than ever.

Johnson, an extremely durable player, played from 1965 through 1976. He then finished his career in Cincinnati.

This is another position where the Browns had much talent. But my second-team tackles are Jerry Sherk and Don Colo.

Sherk was a superb player until an injury and surgery ended his career. Colo filled the role of "enforcer" for the Browns. Colo, out of Brown University, became a different person when he took out his teeth and went to work on Sunday afternoons.

I must mention Lou Rymkus. He could go both ways at tackle and often did in the early days of his career.

### Linebackers
**CLAY MATTHEWS, BILL WILLIS, JIM HOUSTON**

Matthews and Newsome are the only current players to be selected for this all-time greats team, although some players may make it in the future. Matthews probably is the Browns' best linebacker ever. He is above most other Browns at the position. He just does everything so well.

Willis was so good that he already is in the Hall of Fame, but he probably could be there at several positions. His speed and quickness are best-suited for linebacker, where he probably would be used by a present-day coach.

Houston was switched from end to outside linebacker after he came to the Browns from Ohio State. Houston was not only intelligent, he also was a strong player.

My second-team linebackers, who did more than win their letters during long careers, are Galen Fiss, Vince Costello and Tony Adamle.

### Defensive Backs
**BERNIE PARRISH, WARREN LAHR, TOMMY JAMES, CLARENCE SCOTT**

James and Lahr were early Browns, both former area players. James played at Massillon High School and Ohio State. Lahr came out of West Wyoming, Pa., to play at Western Reserve before joining the Browns. Both were excellent technicians with top athletic skills. They also were two of the most personable players to play for the Cleveland team.

Parrish was like having a coach on the field. Some players from the 1964 championship team credit him with designing the defense that shut down John Unitas and the Baltimore Colts.

Scott is a more modern-era player but one who could play any position in the backfield. He ended his career with 39 interceptions and also was a longtime captain of the team.

My second-team defensive backs are Thom Darden, Don Paul, Erich Barnes and Ross Fichtner. How do today's Dawgs—Hanford Dixon and Frank Minnifield—rate? I'll tell you in a few years.

## SPECIAL TEAMS

*Punter*
**HORACE GILLOM**

This young man from Massillon joined the team in 1947 and was the punter for 10 years. He boomed the ball long and high, and there were few good returns.

Gillom, who also played as a wide receiver, was pushed for this all-time team honor by Don Cockroft, an outstanding punter and place-kicker. It wasn't until Cockroft had left that the Browns realized just how fortunate the team was to have someone able to fill both spots so well for such a long time.

*Place-Kicker*
**LOU GROZA**

The Toe was an incomparable clutch kicker. His teammates felt that his kicks were automatic and they usually were right. He still holds 14 Browns records and finished his career with 1,349 points.

Don Cockroft comes in second again as place-kicker, but he would have been a first-team all-timer on many NFL teams. He consistently reached the end zone with his kickoffs and was deadly on field goals from inside the 40-yard line.

*Kick Returner*

**LEROY KELLY**

Kelly, like Groza, is a first-team all-timer at two positions. He led the NFL in punt returns and averaged 25 yards on 48 kick-offs in his first two pro seasons. Then he filled Jim Brown's shoes as the workhorse in the Browns' backfield. He was a great all-around talent.

His backup is Dino Hall, now a high school teacher and coach, who had great speed and the burning desire to succeed. A small man, Hall was a constant threat to go all the way to the end zone.

## THE COACH

**PAUL BROWN**

This may be the easiest choice. P.B., as he is known to his friends, is in the Hall of Fame as a coach, and he deserves it. He organized and coached the original Browns and brought many innovations to the game. After being fired in Cleveland, he went to California, then returned to football to build the Cincinnati Bengals into the powerful team it is today.

My choice for second-team coach is Blanton Collier, a long-time assistant to Brown, who knew as much football as anyone I've met. He could tutor any position and often did. He brought the team its last title in 1964 and retired early because of a hearing problem.

## HONORABLE MENTION

Selecting the cream of the crop of the Browns wasn't easy. There are so many players just below the all-time category that I want to single out some for honorable mention.

They include: Dick Ambrose, Chip Banks, Maurice Bassett, Darrell Brewster. Tom Catlin, Monte Clark, Ben Davis, John Demarie, Don Fleming, Bobby Franklin, John Garlington, Ernie

Green, Charlie Hall, Fred Hoaglin, Lin Houston, Dub Jones, Jim Kanicki, Ernie Kellermann, John Kissell, Ken Konz, Rich Kreitling, Dale Lindsey, Mike Lucci, Walter Michaels, Dick Modzelewski, Ed Modzelewski, John Morrow, Bill Nelsen, Chuck Noll, Floyd Peters, Frank Pitts, Greg Pruitt, Mike Pruitt, Ray Renfro, Walter (The Flea) Roberts, Reggie Rucker, Frank Ryan, Lou Rymkus, John Sandusky, Henry Sheppard, Walt Sumner, Tommy Thompson and Ed Ulinski.

So there they are—the best of the Browns. This group with tremendous football talent provided the city with many exciting times.

# About the Author

CHUCK HEATON EARNED A spot in the Pro Football Hall of Fame in Canton, Ohio. He is one of a select group of writers to receive the prestigious Dick McCann Memorial Award, awarded to one journalist each year for a lifetime of excellence in football reporting. He received the award in 1980 while still actively reporting on the Cleveland Browns for the *Plain Dealer*.

Heaton began writing as a city reporter for the *Plain Dealer* in 1942, earning $50 a week, and stayed with the paper for 51 years. In 1946 he eagerly accepted a job writing in the sports department, where he covered the Cleveland Indians for several years, including a World Series. In 1954 he began covering the Browns as a football writer, a position he filled until 1993.

Heaton was one of the first electors to the Hall of Fame in 1963 and served in that role for thirty years. In 1990 he received the Lifetime Achievement Award from the Cleveland Chapter of the Society of Professional Journalists. He was elected to the Cleveland Journalism Hall of Fame in 1992. He retired from the *Plain Dealer* on October 1, 1993.

He was chosen by Leroy Kelly to be his presenter when Kelly was inducted into the Hall of Fame in 1994.

Heaton's lifelong emphasis on faith and family, and a love of reading, writing and the arts, are reflected in the lives of his five adult children.

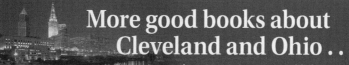

# More good books about Cleveland and Ohio . . .

*from* **Gray & Company, Publishers**

## SPORTS - FOOTBALL

**Browns Town 1964** / The remarkable story of the upstart AFC Cleveland Browns' surprise championship win over the hugely favored Baltimore Colts. *Terry Pluto* / $14.95 softcover

**Heart of a Mule** / Former Browns and OSU Buckeye player, Dick Schafrath retells many wild and entertaining stories from his life. *Dick Schafrath* / $24.95 hardcover

**The Toe** / No one played longer for the Browns. Relive the golden era of pro football in this autobiography by Lou "The Toe" Groza. *with Mark Hodermarsky* / $12.95 softcover

**On Being Brown** / Thoughtful and humorous essays and interviews with legendary Browns players ponder what it means to be a true Browns fan. *Scott Huler* / $12.95 softcover

**False Start** / A top sports journalists takes a hard look at the new Browns franchise and tells how it was set up to fail. *Terry Pluto* / $19.95 hardcover

## SPORTS - BASEBALL

**The Top 20 Moments in Cleveland Sports** Twenty exciting stories recount the most memorable and sensational events in Cleveland sports history. *Bob Dyer* / $14.95 softcover

**Ask Hal** / Answers to fans' most interesting questions about baseball rules from a Hall of Fame sportswriter. *Hal Lebovitz* / $14.95 softcover

**The Curse of Rocky Colavito** / The classic book about the Cleveland Indians' amazing era of futility: 1960-1993. *Terry Pluto* / $14.95 softcover

**Whatever Happened to "Super Joe"?** / Catch up with 45 good old guys from the bad old days of the Cleveland Indians. *Russell Schneider* / $14.95 softcover

**Dealing** / A behind-the-scenes look at the Cleveland Indians front office that tells how and why trades and other deals are made to build the team. *Terry Pluto* / $24.95 hardcover

**Our Tribe** / A father, a son, and the relationship they shared through their mutual devotion to the Cleveland Indians. *Terry Pluto* / $14.95 softcover

**Omar!** / All-Star shortstop Omar Vizquel retells his life story on and off the field in this candid baseball memoir. Includes 41 color photos. *With Bob Dyer* / $14.95 softcover

## SPORTS - GENERAL

**Best of Hal Lebovitz** / A collection of great sportswriting from six decades, by the late dean of Cleveland sportswriters. *Hal Lebovitz* / $24.95 hardcover

**Curses! Why Cleveland Sports Fans Deserve to Be Miserable** / A collection of a lifetime of tough luck, bad breaks, goofs, and blunders. *Tim Long* / $9.95 softcover

**LeBron James: The Rise of a Star** / From high school hoops to #1 NBA draft pick, an inside look at the life and early career of basketball's hottest young star. *David Lee Morgan Jr.* / $14.95 softcover

**Heroes, Scamps & Good Guys** / 101 profiles of the most colorful characters from Cleveland sports history. Will rekindle memories for any Cleveland sports fan. *Bob Dolgan* / $24.95 hardcover

**The View from Pluto** / Award-winning sportswriter Terry Pluto's best columns about Northeast Ohio sports from 1990–2002. *Terry Pluto* / $14.95 softcover

**Cleveland Golfer's Bible** / All of Greater Cleveland's golf courses and driving ranges described in detail. Essential guide for any golfer. *John H. Tidyman* / $13.95 softcover

**Golf Getaways from Cleveland** / 50 great golf trips just a short car ride from home. Plan easy weekends, business meetings, reunions, other gatherings. *John H. Tidyman* / $14.95 softcover

## HISTORY & NOSTALGIA

**Cleveland Rock & Roll Memories** / Revisit the glory days of rock & roll in Cleveland. *Carlo Wolff* / $19.95 softcover

**Strange Tales from Ohio** / Offbeat tales about the Buckeye State's most remarkable people, places, and events. *Neil Zurcher* / $13.95 softcover

**Cleveland Food Memories** / A nostalgic look back at the food we loved, the places we bought it, and the people who made it special. *Gail Ghetia Bellamy* / $17.95 softcover

**Cleveland Amusement Park Memories** A nostalgic look back at Euclid Beach Park, Puritas Springs Park, Geauga Lake Park, and other classic parks. *David & Diane Francis* / $19.95 softcover

**Barnaby and Me** / Linn Sheldon, a Cleveland TV legend as "Barnaby," tells the fascinating story of his own extraordinary life. / $12.95 softcover

**The Cleveland Orchestra Story** / How a midwestern orchestra became a titan in the world of classical music. With 102 rare photographs. *Donald Rosenberg* / $40.00 hardcover

**Finding Your Family History** / Practical how-to with detailed instructions to help find the roots to your family tree in Northeast Ohio. *Vicki Blum Vigil* / $19.95 softcover

**Ghoulardi** / The behind-the-scenes story of Cleveland's wildest TV legend. Rare photos, interviews, show transcripts, and Ghoulardi trivia. *Tom Feran & R. D. Heldenfels* / $17.95 softcover

**Whatever Happened to the "Paper Rex" Man?** / Nostalgic essays and photos rekindle memories of Cleveland's Near West Side neighborhood. *The May Dugan Center* / $15.95 softcover

**Ohio Road Trips** / Discover 52 of Neil Zurcher's all-time favorite Ohio getaways. *Neil Zurcher* / $13.95 softcover

**Cleveland Ethnic Eats** / The guide to authentic ethnic restaurants and markets in Northeast Ohio. *Laura Taxel* / $13.95 softcover

**52 Romantic Outings in Greater Cleveland** / Easy-to-follow "recipes" for romance —a lunch hour, an evening, or a full day together. *Miriam Carey* / $13.95 softcover

**Great Inn Getaways from Cleveland** / 58 distinctive inns & hotels perfect for a weekend or an evening away from home. *Doris Larson* / $14.95 softcover

**Bed & Breakfast Getaways from Cleveland** / 80 charming small inns, perfect for an easy weekend or evening away from home. *Doris Larson* / $14.95 softcover

**Ohio Oddities** / An armchair guide to the offbeat, way out, wacky, oddball, and otherwise curious roadside attractions of the Buckeye State. *Neil Zurcher* / $13.95 softcover

**Cleveland Cops** / Sixty cops tell gritty and funny stories about patrolling the streets of Cleveland. *John H. Tidyman* / $14.95 paperback

**Amy: My Search for Her Killer** / Secrets and suspects in the unsolved murder of Amy Mihaljevic. *James Renner* / $24.95 hardcover

**They Died Crawling**
**The Maniac in the Bushes**
**The Corpse in the Cellar**
**The Killer in the Attic**
**Death Ride at Euclid Beach**
Five collections of gripping true tales about notable Cleveland crimes and disasters. Includes photos. / $13.95 softcover (each)

**Women Behaving Badly** / 16 strange-but-true tales of Cleveland's most ferocious female killers. *John Stark Bellamy II* / $24.95 hardcover

**The Milan Jacovich mystery series** / Cleveland's favorite private eye solves tough cases in these 13 popular detective novels. *Les Roberts* / $13.95 (each) softcover

**We'll Always Have Cleveland** / The memoir of mystery novelist Les Roberts, his character Milan Jacovich, and the city of Cleveland. *Les Roberts* / $24.95 hardcover

**Cleveland on Foot / Beyond Cleveland on Foot** / Great hikes and self-guided walking tours in and around Greater Cleveland and 7 neighboring counties. *Patience Cameron Hoskins, with Rob & Peg Bobel* / $15.95 (each) softcover

**Cleveland Fishing Guide** / Best public fishing spots in Northeast Ohio, what kind of fish you'll find, and how to catch them. Directory of fishing resources. *John Barbo* / $14.95 softcover

**Dick Goddard's Weather Guide for Northeast Ohio** / Seasonal facts, folklore, storm tips, and weather from Cleveland's top meteorologist. / $13.95 softcover

**Cleveland: A Portrait of the City** / 105 color photographs capture Greater Cleveland's landmarks and hidden details in all seasons. *Jonathan Wayne* / $35.00 hardcover

**Truth & Justice for Fun & Profit** / Collected newspaper reporting from 25 years by the *Plain Dealer's* Michael Heaton. / $24.95 hardcover

**Full of It** / Strong words and fresh thinking for Cleveland by *Plain Dealer* columnist Sam Fulwood. *Sam Fulwood III* / $24.95 hardcover

**Is It Just Me?** / Columnist Dick Feagler pulls no punches in this collection of hard-hitting *Plain Dealer* columns. / $24.95 hardcover

**"I know I'm not supposed to say this . . . But I'll say it anyway."** / More controversial recent columns by Dick Feagler, dean of Cleveland newspaper columnists. / $22.95 hardcover

**Feagler's Cleveland / "Did You Read Feagler Today?"** / The best and most talked about columns from three decades of commentary by Cleveland's top columnist, Dick Feagler. / $13.95 softcover (each)

**Faith and You** / 28 short essays on finding faith to face each day and trying to live that day the right way. *Terry Pluto* / $19.95 hardcover

**Everyday Faith** / Practical essays on personal faith and the ethical choices we face in everyday life. *Terry Pluto* / $19.95 hardcover

**What's So Big About Cleveland, Ohio?** 10-year-old Amanda expects to be bored visiting Cleveland—until she makes an exciting discovery. Illustrated children's book. *Sara Holbrook* / $17.95